Tom Watson's
Strategic Golf

Tom Watson's Strategic Golf

Tom Watson
with Nick Seitz

Illustrated by
Anthony Ravielli

POCKET BOOKS

New York   London   Toronto   Sydney   Tokyo   Singapore

Published by:

NYT Special Services, Inc.
A New York Times Company,
5520 Park Avenue, Box 395
Trumbull, CT 06611-0395

and

POCKET BOOKS, a division of Simon & Schuster Inc.
1230 Avenue of the Americas
New York, NY 10020

Book Design by Laura Hough

Illustrations by Anthony Ravielli

ISBN: 0-671-74362-7

First NYT Special Services, Inc. and Pocket Books
hardcover printing July 1993

10   9   8   7   6   5   4   3   2   1

Printed in the U.S.A.

To Nick Seitz:

*A man with whom I have shared a lot of laughs and
a man who takes his deadlines seriously.
I really appreciate you.*

Tom Watson

CONTENTS

ACKNOWLEDGMENTS

The authors thank the following for their unstinting help in producing this book. They prove that computers are useful but people are invaluable. We couldn't have done it without the gracious support of, in alphabetical order: Kelly Fray, who schedules Tom Watson's activities; Doug Hardy, who oversaw the project for the Golf Digest books department; the ever-energetic Linda Hipski, who typed and input the manuscript among many other assignments; Laura Hough, who did the clear and appealing design; Hope Johnson, a doggedly rigorous copy editor, and Mary Rung, who coordinated the production aspects and by the end was talking golf almost like a veteran.

FOREWORD
by Fred Couples

I felt really honored to be asked to write the foreword for this book, because I consider Tom Watson one of the finest strategists in golf. Ever. You hear a lot about different players from the past and how they had a plan for what they were going to do before they went out and played a single hole. I wish I had had the opportunity to see Ben Hogan firsthand and talk to him about his strategy for attacking a golf course, but I've been fortunate to play with and against Tom Watson for a lot of years, and I repeatedly have seen up close why he is such a great player.

One of the keys, I believe, is that he never gets flustered on the course, and the reason is because he thinks things through. He never lets outside factors—like the way he just played the previous hole—dictate the way he plays the next hole. I really believe there have been tournaments where he has thought through every single shot he was going to play. Emotion doesn't come into it. His temper doesn't take over. His strategy is set before the game even starts.

That really separates him, and that kind of mental toughness can be learned. Tom is the best man to teach it. That's one of the reasons this book is so important to golfers of all levels.

Just before I started on a really good stretch of play leading up to the 1992 Masters, I visited Tom in Kansas City to try to learn more about how he prepares for tournaments. It was one of the smartest things I've done. He got two very important points through to me: You have to stay focused on the job for the last nine holes, because you've spent 63 holes getting to that point; and you must stay within yourself and avoid trying shots you're not capable of and haven't practiced.

Watching Tom in dozens of tournaments, I can tell you those are principles he sticks to in his own play. I know this is why he was able to win five British Opens, the tournament that takes as much strategy, if not more, than any other. I remember watching him at Troon, and he needed a birdie to tie on the last hole. Some guys would have tried to take a longer club and blow it down there off the tee—and risk hitting it in the bunkers. He hit the same club he had hit the three days before, a 1-iron. He didn't make birdie that time, but he gave himself a chance by sticking to his plan. And that's why he's won eight majors and 32 tournaments and been Player of the Year half a dozen times.

He's so good because he's unfazed by whomever he's playing and by the circumstances. Those traits haven't changed throughout his career. He's been fearless and he's got a game plan. These two work together. When you're prepared, you're more confident. When you have a strategy, you're more comfortable.

Here's a personal example. I played better in 1992 mainly because I attacked the par 5s more strategically. I learned to lay up and wedge it to the green, and then I made a lot of 12-foot putts for birdies. The first half of the year I birdied about three-quarters of the par 5s. I can hit the ball plenty far, but I raised my game a level when I stopped trying to overpower the golf course and started thinking more like Tom.

I'm glad Tom has written this book. I'm sure I'll be able to pick up a few more tips from him myself. And I know it will really be a help to the player who hasn't thought enough about course strategy before. It might even make you a winner.

PREFACE
by Nick Seitz

I have been collaborating on Golf Digest material and books with Tom Watson for more than 15 years now, and I can say without equivocation he is the best caddie I have ever had. I always play several strokes better when he picks my clubs and charts my course. You will too once you absorb the thinking in this book.

It's one thing to learn to swing by watching a superstar. It's quite another to climb inside his head and learn from his thought processes. Watson gives us that privileged access in the next 100-plus pages. The longer I'm around this bedeviling game, the more I realize that the very best players are the very best strategists. They beat you with their minds as much as with their drivers and putters. Watson has always been known for his fast-paced, exciting style—but underpinning that style is rigorously intellectual planning. He defines his options on every shot, weighs the variables, plays the shot decisively.

Over the years he has developed strategic rules to live by, some of them memorable. He wants us to "straighten out a dogleg on the tee," and shows us how to do that. He shows us how to position ourselves to "shoot up the length of the green" on approach shots. He explains why it's better to "work the ball into a wall of wind" than to ride a crosswind.

In this book Watson plays us through dozens of different situations, some well known and some not, and explains the varying possibilities for different kinds of players. Slicers (call us power faders) get special attention because we predominate. Watson believes we need to allow for our chronic slices much more thoughtfully.

Books on the full swing would pile higher than the tallest mountain. Books on strategy barely reach the top of a ball washer. It's time for a book of tactics by an all-time great, a psychology major from Stanford whose mental acuity is a major reason he may prove the last American superstar.

Eddie Merrins, one of our premier teaching professionals, says strategy is the next frontier in golf. "This is the cutting edge," he says. "Most teaching leaves you on the practice tee. The golf course is a different world. A Tom Watson knows that well."

Watson loves a lively wager, and passes along his tips on match play and betting toward the end of the book. He does not relate how Jim Hansberger of Ram Golf and I plucked him a few years ago, however, and I thought you might want to know in case you ever find yourself trying to win Watson's money.

After five holes of a rather dull nine, Watson proposed a little action to enliven the proceedings. "I'll play from your worst drive for the rest of the nine, and you play my drive—for a dollar," he said. "It's the honor system—you have to do your best."

The sixth hole at the Greenbrier's Old White Course, where the match began, is the No. 1 handicap hole, a 434-yard par 4. Hansberger drove spectacularly for our side, 83 yards into the rough, from where Watson could not reach the green. Watson drove 275 up the middle.

Given that powerful head start, I eventually chipped close and made the putt for par, while Watson two-putted for bogey. Hackers quickly lead, 1 up.

Hansberger again drove splendidly on the 380-yard seventh hole, just clearing a culvert in the right rough and leaving Watson a long shot from behind a tree. Watson drove 275 up the middle.

Both Hansberger and I missed the green to the left, from where Jim got up and down for par. Watson hit an impressive low slice around the tree with a 2-iron, but the ball skittered across the green and into the trees beyond. His eyes aglare, Watson took forever sizing up his recovery possibilities. He finally played a bump-and-run shot about as well as he could have, but it caught a downslope and finished 35 feet on the other side of the hole. Treating the putt as if it were for the British Open instead of a dollar, he rapped it in for a saving halve and muttered, "If I had to hit from where you guys do all the time, I think I'd give up the bleeping game."

Hackers still lead 1 up.

The eighth hole is a 190-yard par 3, uphill, and the wind was against us. I assaulted the ball with a 3-iron and put it on the far edge of the green, a long way from the hole. Hansberger pulled out a 5-wood.

"What do you have there?" asked Watson.

Hansberger told him.

"You gotta be kidding. I'm clubbing you. Take a 4-wood."

I lodged a protest, ignored by Watson.

Hansberger hit the green with the 4-wood.

Everyone made par, one hole to go, hackers lead 1 up.

The ninth is 400 yards, into the wind, with a fairway squeezed by bunkers in the long driving area. Hansberger unfortunately drove respectably.

I lined up and Watson said, "Aim more to the right."

"Why?"

"Because you dead-pulled your last two drives."

I lined up more to the right, timed my downswing lurch closely and met the ball almost solidly, exclaiming "Oh no!" as I swung into what passes for my follow-through. The "Oh no!" went 230 yards in the fairway.

Watson, to his credit, rocketed his drive—into the wind, mind you—100 yards straight past mine. He hit a middle iron onto the green, we hit wedges onto the green and all three of us two-putted for pars. Hackers win, 1 up.

Not many weeks later, Watson forwarded to me a rather bedraggled-looking dollar bill. I sent it back, requesting a personal check signed and suitable for framing. So far he has not responded.

INTRODUCTION
by Tom Watson

Playing strategic golf is a matter of negotiating with yourself. You have to negotiate how much risk you are going to take and whether the potential reward is worth it. Most holes offer a safe route and a dangerous route. The safe route probably will be longer and may involve laying up, but it will avoid hazards. The dangerous route is potentially more rewarding, but if you don't hit good shots you may well make a double bogey or worse. The greater the risk, the greater the reward.

Every shot has its own risk/reward factor. Everybody is tempted to take chances, to go right at the flag. But you have to negotiate a sensible attitude with yourself. You have to recognize problems and play percentages. What are your odds of making a long carry over water from a poor lie? If you realistically can't make the shot eight or nine times in 10, your odds are poor. Coin-toss odds aren't good enough. Grade the degree of risk—is the shot impossible, very difficult, moderately difficult?

Every once in a while you will bring off a few heroic shots and score better than usual. But over the course of an entire season, you will lower your handicap and win more bets if you discipline yourself to avoid risks. Your game won't be as exciting as going hell-bent for great shots and hitting the ball as hard as you can, but you'll be more successful—and isn't that the object?

To judge your risk/reward possibilities intelligently, you have to know your strengths and weaknesses. Play to your strengths and away from your weaknesses. If a bunker is on your line to the flag, you should look at that bunker very differently depending on whether you are a good bunker player or a bad bunker player. If you are a bad bunker player, you'd better aim away from the bunker, no matter if you'll have a longer putt or even be in the rough. You need to learn to make "good misses."

I've always been a good bunker player, so I might deliberately hit into the bunker if I'm playing a shot out of the trees that I couldn't stop on the green or that would be in heavy rough if I came up short. I'll have a better chance of getting up and down from the bunker.

Every shot is a guess. Your challenge is to make it as educated a guess as possible. A 100-shooter can learn to enjoy all the lively decision-making the par-shooter can. That's what makes the game enjoyable. There's satisfaction in knowing your thinking was on target, even if your shot wasn't.

FORGET THESE CLUBS

I like to play with average golfers and help them think their way around the course. If I were caddieing for most of you, the first thing I would do is take half a dozen clubs out of your bag. I'd never let you hit them if you were playing for score.

I'd start by removing the driver, which most of you hit too low and slice too much. Freddie Couples found he can drive better with a 3-wood, a club he "borrowed" from me. Chuck Cook, who teaches Payne Stewart as well as many average players, cites research showing that unless you can swing the club at least 85 miles per hour, the 3-wood actually carries farther than the driver! Cook says you must be able to carry your driver 170 yards in the air or there is no good reason to pack one. (The only time the driver would be better is when conditions give you a lot more roll.) The 3-wood gives you much greater accuracy.

I'd probably eliminate your long irons down to a 5-iron. Irons are being made so strong these days, a 4-iron has become a long iron. And, to play for score, I'd probably have you hit your 5-iron off the tee a half-dozen times during the round. Many times when you know you can't reach a green anyway, you will keep the ball in play better with shorter clubs, avoiding danger and controlling your shots.

On every shot I'd remind you to consider all the variables: your lie, the wind, elevation, where the flag is on the green, how you feel, how you're hitting the ball on a given day. No two shots are the same. Inform yourself as fully as possible before you hit any shot.

Always play a shot with the next shot in mind. Golf is like chess. You have to think ahead, at least one move and often more than one. Plot the hole back from the flag. Learn the locations of the flags. If you drive your car past two or three holes arriving at the course, note where the flags are. If you are playing a hole and walk past another hole you will play later, note the flag.

Every hole is a little tournament of its own. Don't look ahead to the next hole or reflect on how your total score is progressing. Stay focused on the hole you're playing. Playing that hole well is your goal.

Don't think too much about your swing on the course. Try to forget mechanics and think tactics. Let your swing happen and it will be drawn to your target.

STUDY BETTER PLAYERS

Watch better players and see how they attack holes. Play with better players whenever you can. I remember when I first came on the PGA Tour and was playing a satellite tournament near the Heritage Classic at Harbour Town. I played my round in the morning and then went over to follow Jack Nicklaus for 18 holes in the big tournament in the afternoon. He's the best strategist I've ever seen, and Harbour Town is a great course. I learned a lot that afternoon. Jack almost never makes a low-percentage shot. He plays the right shot for any situation.

I use Nicklaus examples in this book. I also use examples from playing Augusta National, because you watch it on television every year and it's a classic strategic course. I'll pass along rules of thumb that help me, such as "Don't miss the green on the flag side."

I was talking recently with a 14-handicap friend about playing Winged Foot. The greens there are firm, fast and slopey. Deep bunkers are cut into the sides of the greens. My game plan for approach shots there is never to miss the green on the side the flag is on. It's too tough to recover.

If the flag's on the right near a difficult bunker, I'm happy with a shot on the left half of the green.

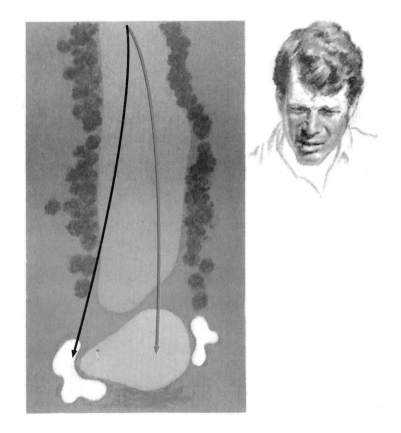

If the flag is on the right, close to a bad bunker, I'm satisfied with a shot anywhere on the left half of the green. I'm taking most of the risk out of the shot, and I'll still have a birdie putt.

My friend said this kind of thinking would serve weekend golfers well on any course, and I have to agree. Try never to miss the green on the flag side.

My overall intent is to heighten your awareness. I want to teach you how to analyze a shot and use your imagination. I want to teach you to understand and then play within your limitations. You'll play better, believe me. You're intelligent readers, but you need to think better on the golf course.

Harvey Penick, the grand old teacher, has the right idea when he says not to worry when you have a bad round. That happens. If you play two bad rounds in a row, hit some balls on the range. Play three bad rounds in a row and you'd better start thinking about making changes in your game. The point is you aren't going to play a good round every time out. Don't give up on proper thinking because it doesn't work one day. Stick with it. You'll be glad you did.

Never lose sight of the fact golf is a game. It is going to test you, but the test is a game. We all take it too seriously at times. If you aren't playing well, the game isn't as much fun. When that happens I tell myself just to go out and play the game as I did when I was a kid.

In summary, most of the thoughts I am about to relate to you in the rest of this book have been taught before. I've learned from Dad, Sam, Bobby, Byron, Stan, Jack, David and others. I hope in writing this book I have done justice to all of them. And for you, the reader, I hope I will have made the game of golf easier to understand and more fun to play.

CHAPTER 1
How Would You Play This Shot?

L et's start the book with a strategy problem. We'll come back to it at the end and compare solutions. By the time you finish the book I expect you to be able to identify and evaluate your several options in the situation shown on the next two pages.

You are facing a second shot on a long par 4 or short par 5. You are in the left side of the fairway, 195 yards from the front edge of the green, 200 yards from the flag, which is cut on the front of the green. You have 170 yards to carry the rock-walled water hazard on line to the flag. It's 60 yards to the left fairway bunker, with plenty of fairway over the bunker. The fairway lay-up area is about 50 yards wide.

Please turn the page to decide which shot to play. We will revisit your strategic options in Chapter 17.

You have 170 yards to carry the water hazard, 200 to the flag. Rate your options.

CHAPTER 2
How to Control and Work the Ball

G ood strategy demands good control of the ball.
Different players and teachers use different methods for maneuvering the ball. My basic method is based on simplicity.

You don't have to be a low handicapper to hit a low hook or a high slice. I'll ask you to make no adjustments in your swing. I rarely make

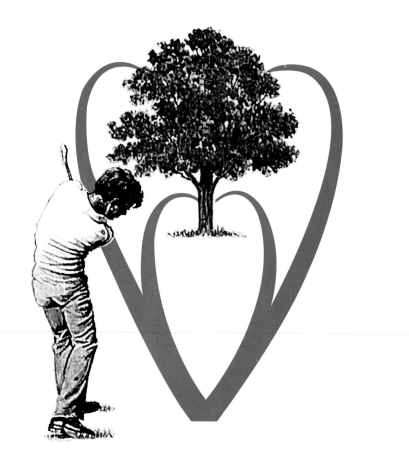

them myself. I don't change my grip except for exaggerated instances.

The benefits of knowing how to shape your shots are several. First, you can change your basic pattern once and for all, from a slice to a hook, for example. You can avoid an obstacle like a tree; you can play a dogleg hole the way the architect designed it; you can get the ball closer to a tight pin position.

It's harder to spin today's balls, but you still can shape your shots, and frequently need to. I try to make every shot fall left or fall right—a straight shot's an accident.

We'll start by talking about the hook and slice, then the high and low shots. Finally, we'll put those elements together to hit the low slice, high slice, low hook and high hook. Then we'll talk about problem-solving. You'll find that expanding your shotmaking ability is extremely useful—and great fun!

To curve the ball, I align my body well away from the target, aim the clubface at the target, and make a normal swing along my stance line. I align my body before I aim the clubface. Once my body is aligned away from the target, I rest the club on the ground (assuming I'm not in a hazard), square the clubface to the target, and take a normal grip. Your ball position should be normal, even though changing your stance may make it appear to change. The ball starts out along the stance line and then curves to the target.

HOW TO SLICE—ON PURPOSE

Most of you slice and don't want to, but at least this will help you understand why. To cut the ball, I align my body left of target and aim the clubface at the target, then swing to the left, along my stance line.

The face, in effect, is open and cuts across the ball to impart slice spin. Do not let the toe of the club pass the heel through impact.

HOW TO HOOK

You pretty much can infer from the above slicing segment how I hook the ball. I align my body—shoulders, hips, knees, feet—to the right of the target, aim the clubface at the target, and swing out to the right.

I make a normal swing along my stance line and control the shape of the shot through the angle of the clubface. The face comes into the ball in a closed position and delivers hook spin.

If you're a chronic slicer, you may have to align your body farther to the right than you think to hit a hook. And you may have to aim at the left rough off the tee to get the ball in the fairway with your slice until you master this approach.

To slice and hook intentionally (facing page), aim your club-face at the target but align your body away from the target.

It also can help the chronic slicer to position the hands more ahead of the ball at address and think about making the toe of the club pass the heel through the impact area.

HOW TO HIT IT LOW

Hitting the ball low is primarily a matter of ball position. I move the ball back in my stance.

Moving the ball back reduces the effective loft of the club. Be aware that when you move the ball back you must square your clubface to the target, because your normal clubface position would now be open. I don't consciously adjust my weight distribution. This follows from the ball position.

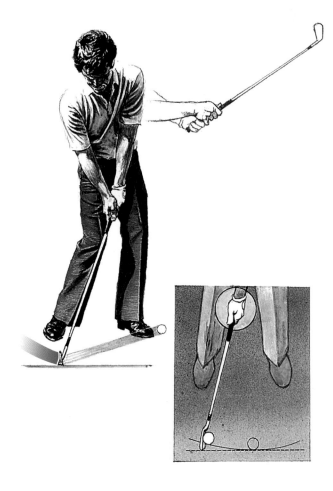

For a low shot I try to finish my swing low.

A key point: Play the ball an inch or so closer to your body on low and high shots or you'll hit the ball on the toe of the club. The correct path of the club comes from inside the target line to along the line to back inside, and when you move the ball forward or backward, the center of the clubface swings into the ball inside the line unless you adjust.

HOW TO HIT IT HIGH

I move the ball forward in my stance, adding loft to the clubface, to hit it higher. As with the low shot, I make sure I square the clubface to the target.

Moving the ball up toward your front foot encourages a higher swing finish, and I strive to finish high with my arms. I also want to stay back with my upper body on the downswing.

Hitting the ball high, I select one more club than usual—a 6-iron instead of a 7-iron, for example—and more than that into the wind, because I'll lose distance. Of course, I still make sure I can clear any obstacle in my path.

Play the ball an inch closer to your body.

If you're worried about hitting the ball high enough, set your left thumb straight down the shaft or even a little left of that. I said I wouldn't change your grip yet, but this simple move almost always guarantees a more lofted clubface.

HOOK IT LOW

This is a comparatively easy shot. Just smother-hook it. Put the ball back in your stance, align your body to the right and your clubface at the target, and swing normally along your stance line.

Let the club release, making the toe of the club pass the heel through impact. Finish low.

Be sure you select a club with enough loft to get the ball airborne.

HOOK IT HIGH

This one's tougher. You really have to release the club and finish high.

Put the ball forward in your stance, align your body to the right, aim the clubface at the target and swing out to the right. Keep your head behind the ball on the downswing and feel that you are releasing the club-head out and up.

An important aid to that kind of release and follow-through is to take the clubhead away from the ball quite low.

SLICE IT LOW

Another true tester. The difficulty is keeping the ball down. I'll put the ball back a bit in my stance to keep from hitting it too high. Gripping down on the club also helps.

Align your body left, aim the clubface at the target, and swing along your stance line. I "block it" hard with my hands—retaining the wrist break on the downswing and making sure the toe of the club does not—repeat, not—pass the heel through the ball.

Finish your swing very low and left, pulling your arms across your body and shutting off your follow-through.

SLICE IT HIGH

Most golfers would prefer to be rid of this shot, and maybe you already know too much about it. Just be sure to keep the clubface open going through the ball.

Position the ball forward and an inch closer to you than normal, with the same body and clubface position as for the low slice. Keep your head back. Finish high and left.

CHANGE YOUR GRIP FOR TROUBLE SHOTS

When I face a trouble shot where I have to slice or hook the ball a lot, I will change my grip. Actually it's probably the easiest way for most players to

*Keep your head
behind the ball to slice
it high.*

G. Ravielli

stop slicing and start to hook the ball. And changing your grip in practice is an excellent way to learn about spin and train yourself in trouble shots.

To hit a major slice, rotate your hands counterclockwise on the grip. To hit a large hook, rotate your hands clockwise. Do NOT rotate the clubhead as you rotate your hands. Many people will strengthen their grips to hit a hook—and set the club down behind the ball with the face rotated open. They defeat their purpose. Leave the club aimed where it was, then just relax your hands and rotate them the way you want to.

The position of the left thumb is central here. If you want to slice the ball, your left thumb should be straight down the top of the club or even a little left of that, in a weak grip. To hook the ball, set your left thumb well over to the right and more under the club. That's an extra strong grip.

Make some swings both ways. It will probably feel terribly awkward. But try to make contact and see what the ball does. When your hands are in a very weak position, the ball will go short, high and to the right. When your hands are in a very strong position, the ball will go lower, longer and left. This happens almost regardless of your swing path. (Normally I'd rather see most of you use a fairly strong grip than a weak one.)

Try this experiment. Set up normally. Start with your thumb down the top of the shaft. That's a weak, good-player's grip. Now move your grip in 30-degree increments. (When you change your grip, be sure you shift both hands and keep the palms facing.)

Move your grip 30 degrees left of center and hit 10 balls. Do this with a 5-iron. I can overcut a 5-iron at least 50 yards with this grip. The more lofted the club, the less the ball will spin. I couldn't slice it nearly that much with a wedge. Lee Trevino can some times. He's such a superior shotmaker he can take a 5-iron and hit 12 different shots with it. I don't have enough talent to do that.

OK. Now move your grip 30 degrees right of center and hit 10 more balls, then move it 60 degrees right and 90 degrees right. Notice the differences in ball behavior: how far the ball goes, how high, how much it rolls.

You can transfer this knowledge to the golf course when you get behind a tree, for instance. Ultimately you can combine a grip adjustment with the earlier adjustments we made in your aim and alignment to get the ball to your target. Start practicing with normal aim and alignment and evolve into aiming and aligning more left for a big slice and more right for a big hook. The bigger the slice or hook you need, the more you exaggerate everything you're doing. You won't completely succeed on a high percentage of these challenging shots, maybe only two out of 10, but those two good practice shots might help you figure out in four-ball play what to try when it's a do-or-die situation. What if you've been slicing all your life but you have to hook the ball around a tree to have any hope on the hole? You may miss the shot, but at least you know you occasionally have been able to hit that abnormal hook on the practice ground. That feedback is what we're after.

You will improve your understanding of shotmaking and quite possibly improve your basic shot shape. The obvious way to stop slicing is to learn how to hook the ball.

THE TWO THEORIES FOR MANEUVERING THE BALL

I've given you two different theories for shaping your shots. In the first, adjust your stance, aim at the target, and swing along your stance line, leaving your grip alone. In the second, for trouble shots primarily, change your grip, adding adjustments in your aim and alignment as you develop your skill level.

You can choose the theory that works best for you, or arrive at a combination of the two theories depending on the shot you need to hit. You have to practice, but not that much. Just hitting a bucket of balls while changing your grip in 30-degree stages is a good start to understanding ball control.

Learning to work the ball demands no rare talent. It does require comprehension and hitting balls. I like to practice by simulating real-life situations.

PRACTICE SHAPING YOUR SHOTS FALDO'S WAY

Once you know how to maneuver the ball, it's good to try practicing shots that fall left or right rather than straight. (I've learned that the key to staging a clinic is to call the shot after you hit it.)

Nick Faldo practices his shotmaking from about 100 yards behind a tree. He'll bend the ball around the tree from left to right and from right to left, low and high. It's a good way to focus your practice.

Try it from different lies, not just good ones, to learn what you can do with the ball. Can you get the ball in the air trying to hook it out of the rough? Probably not.

Realize when you get on the course that your left-to-right shots generally won't go as far as your right-to-left shots.

ALWAYS USE A SWING THOUGHT

Once you determine the shape of the shot you need to hit, you need a key thought for hitting that shot. It is awfully difficult to have more than one thought involved with the swing, but you need one, and it's better on the course if it relates to the shot.

Most top players rely on a takeaway thought. For instance, if Arnold Palmer wants to cut a shot from left to right, his key probably will be to start the club back outside the target line. I might tell myself to hold the club more firmly with the last three fingers of the left hand. But you need a relevant thought to be a versatile shotmaker.

CHAPTER 3
Club Selection and Judging Distance

Judging distance and picking the right club for the shot are prerequisites for scoring your best. It's no good to be short in the water, and it's little better to be long in a severe bunker.

When my pro-am partners want help judging distance, which they often do, I ask them how far they carry the ball with a particular club. Usually they can't answer—and I can't club them well.

Or they might say they hit the ball 150 yards with a 7-iron. But they did that only once, downwind, downhill and counting 45 feet of roll on a burned-out course. I want to know how far they carry the ball under normal conditions.

There's a lot of sound advice around about pacing off yardages on a practice range, but I'm afraid it isn't very practical. I suggest you pace off exactly how far you hit your shots on a wet course, since you can see where your ball lands and leaves a mark. Par-3 holes present a fine opportunity for measuring club distances.

You have the advantage of working under real conditions. Factor in the wind and you'll have a valid feel for your yardages. The trouble is too many people play in golf carts and can't pace off their shots—or get enough exercise.

Check the length of your stride so you can pace shots accurately. I have short legs. By stretching out a little, my stride is about a yard.

A tour pro, in addition to understanding how far he carries the ball, wants precise shot lengths when he's preparing to hit. My caddie gets my yardages for me by pacing the course and consulting hole diagrams that are given out. You may not have this luxury, but you do need to find out as much as you can about key distances.

Most courses have markers 150 yards from the green. I like marked sprinkler heads because they're on a good angle to the green whereas a bush or stake that's off to the side might not be. But are you 150 from the front of the green or the middle? If a green is 40 yards deep and it's 150 to the middle, then it's 130 to the front and 170 to the back. That's nearly a four-club spread!

Check the length of your stride so you can pace shots accurately. I have short legs. By stretching out a little, my stride is about a yard.

36" Stride

WATSON'S YARDAGES IN THE AIR

Woods:	Driver	3	4	Irons	1	2	3	4	5	6	7	8	9	Wedge
Yards:	250	243	230		225	215	205	195	182	170	156	145	132	120

Pace the distance to your ball mark on a wet course.

150 Yards

I want to know from the caddie how far it is to the front and then how much farther to the hole. If the pin's in front, I want to hear "130 plus 10." I'll probably pick a club to fly the ball onto the front of the green, and let it roll to the hole. If there are no hazards in front, I might land the ball short and run it up, depending on variables like pin position and the firmness of the ground.

If it's 150 to the center and I flew the ball 150, I'd probably go over the green and face a testy, downhill recovery shot coming back. Unless there's severe trouble in front of the green, you are better off being short, because most greens cant from back to front, and an uphill chip or putt is much easier. Most of you come up short more often than not, because you mis-hit the ball to some degree, and that helps you stay short. But I don't want to mislead you into picking weaker clubs when the common failing is to come up too short. Sam Snead always has advised average golfers to take more club because they aren't going to hit many pure shots. Most of you are too vain to listen to him. Sam, ironically, was not a great judge of distance before yardage books became common. He says he'd have won 50 more tournaments if he'd played by yardage his entire career. As it is, he won only enough to set a record that should never be broken.

There's a great anecdote about a 20-handicapper asking Sam how he, the 20-handicapper, could put backspin on his 3-iron shots the way Sam did. Sam asked the fellow how far he hit his 3-iron on average. About 150 yards was the answer. "Then why in hell," wondered Sam, "would you want to put backspin on it?"

Sam was terrific at hitting the ball the right distance when he had a good yardage. You make a lot of birdies by being hole high with your approach shots. When Johnny Miller, now a television announcer, was scorching the tour a few years ago, he hit an amazing number of approaches the right distance. He was probably the best at it I've seen.

It all starts with knowing how far you carry the ball.

I have to know my yardages in the air to make a living at golf. Under normal conditions I know I carry my driver 250 yards, my 1-iron 225, my 5-iron 182, my 8-iron 145 and my pitching wedge 120. I check these distances each year to see if they've changed.

WHEN TO TAKE MORE CLUB

Underclubbing is most common in certain situations. You should be especially aware of the need for using more club in these cases:

1. *When the air is damp.* My normal 7-iron distance is 155 to 160 yards, but in wet, heavy air it's about 150. If I fail to adjust for this loss of

distance, I'll finish some 15 to 30 feet short of the flagstick.

2. *Into a strong headwind.* Most golfers badly underestimate the extent to which a headwind will shorten a shot. Many of you are reluctant to take a stronger club, no matter how hard the wind is blowing. I believe that when the wind velocity is more than 10 miles per hour you should step down at least two clubs stronger. I've often gone down four or five clubs in a rough wind.

3. *Shooting to a raised green.* When the green is elevated, it will interrupt the ball's flight, stopping the shot before it can carry forward as far as it normally would. The higher the green sits above your ball level, the more club you will need.

Often these shot-shortening conditions come in a combined form. Obviously you would really need to make a big adjustment in your club selection if you were about to play a shot to a raised green on a cold, damp day with a strong wind blowing in your face.

STUDY YOUR LIE

The lie of the ball always influences what club you choose. The lie is a primary influence on shotmaking and one that many golfers underestimate. It determines the trajectory and distance of your shot. The worse the lie, the more I'll tend to play the ball back in my stance. Playing the ball back and keeping my hands ahead of the ball through impact will produce a more descending blow and solid contact.

If you are in a bad lie in the rough, obviously you have a problem getting to your intended target. If you are in the fairway in a divot, that's another problem. If you are in the fairway and you have a fluffy lie rather than a clean lie, that's yet another problem. A fluffy lie causes a flyer. The divot causes a lower shot. The heavy rough could cause the shot not even to get near the green.

If the ball is in long grass that lies in the opposite direction of the shot I'm going to play, I'll consciously try to hit the ball harder. Conversely, if the ball is lying downgrain, I'll hit it easier.

So always examine closely the lie of the ball to determine what the ball is likely to do. This makes it much easier to choose the right club for the best results.

WHERE DO YOU WANT YOUR BAD SHOT TO GO?

Determine what the wind is doing. That's easier to do walking than riding in a cart. How will it influence your club selection and shot shape? Do you want the ball to go on the right side or left side of the green? If you habitually slice and the wind is left to right, you'd better aim left of the green. If you hit a bad shot, where do you want your bad shot to go? Wind has a lot to do with that.

Determine if it is an all-or-nothing shot and whether to go for it. It is all or nothing if you must carry the ball long over water. Or if you must try to get it close to that pin on the edge of the green near a deep bunker. These thoughts should go through your mind as you pick a club.

Finally look at the negative aspect—where you don't want the ball to go—and work to the positive aspect from there. That isn't negative thinking. It's planning. You look at the problems and you look at the area you think you can hit with a reasonably good shot 80 percent of the time.

IN BETWEEN CLUBS?

What about when you're caught between clubs? A normal 6-iron will come up short, a normal 5-iron will go too far. What should you do?

I learned from Gene Littler to take the longer club. Then I make one of two adjustments: I shorten my swing, or I grip down on the club.

If I'm playing well I'll be more confident in the shorter swing. You need to have practiced it, though. Gripping down on the club automatically shortens the arc of the swing and lessens the centrifugal force.

The general advantage of swinging the longer club is that you don't have to try to overpower the shot. You can swing firmly but smoothly, with a clear mind. And a clear mind is at least half the battle judging distance and picking the right club.

Here's another tack when you're in between clubs. If a normal 6-iron is not quite enough club and there is a left-to-right wind, I might take that 6-iron and strengthen my grip some, aim a bit to the right of the hole and try to hit a little hook in there. I know the ball is going to go a little farther than it will with my normal 6-iron, and the left-to-right wind will straighten it out so it won't hook too much. I can use a 6-iron with a stronger grip and get the ball to the hole. If I have a hook wind, I wouldn't do that, because the ball would go too far left, coming in at too much of a right-to-left angle to stop on the green.

Or if your club is too strong, weaken your grip a little. If the pin is on the right front of the green, aim to the left side of the green and hit a high fade in there. It comes down softly and stops quickly.

I remember deliberately hitting a very weak shot out of the rough one time at the Anheuser-Busch Classic at Silverado. I had a 120-yard shot and hit a 7-iron out of the rough with a real weak grip. I felt if I tried to hit a 9-iron or 8-iron, I would try to hit it too hard and the ball wouldn't have enough backspin to stop. It would be coming down too hard. I thought to

myself, "Well, why don't I just hit a really weak 7-iron shot like a hacker." It finished about two feet from the hole.

I didn't have to hit it too hard. I did hit it at pretty full speed, but because the grip was so weak, the clubhead didn't turn over through impact, and the ball went high because the clubface was open (I aimed left). I did it to prevent a flyer, and it worked.

Other times I have turned my hands into a stronger grip and hit a hard hook. At the Masters one year, I was in contention and hit my drive around the corner at 13, but not quite far enough to go for the green with a normal 4-wood shot. I had to hook a big second shot around the bend, so I got up there with a 4-wood and turned my hands more under the shaft. I caught the ball solidly and it went out there and hooked about 35 yards. I knew it was going to hook—I was just hoping it was going to hook enough. I started it right of the green and the water.

The ball ended up four feet from the hole. I yipped the eagle putt, but that hook charged me up. Bringing off a shot like that can pick up a round. I went on to birdie the next hole, too.

Picking a club in ever-varying conditions is finally a guess for even the very best players. Golf is an unsettling game. Study your lie, get a good yardage, factor in the wind, assess the problems in your target area and make a positive swing. That's the best any of us can do.

CHAPTER 4
Teeing the Ball

There's more to teeing the ball than you might think.

I've become good friends with Lee Trevino in recent years, and have played a lot of golf with him as he's become a superstar all over again on the U.S. senior tour. You learn by watching good players, and I learned something about teeing the ball from Lee.

Lee's a fader—he likes to curve the ball from left to right—and on a straight hole he will tee up on the right side of the teeing area. Lee is giving himself as much room for error as possible. Teeing up to the right lets him aim more to the left and use more of the fairway with his fade.

If you're one of the millions who slice, you usually should tee up on the right side of the tee. Slicers I know often will tee up on the left side and not aim far enough left. The ball starts out too much toward the center of the fairway and then slices out of play to the right.

If you hook the ball rather than slice it, tee up on the left side of the tee so you can start the ball far enough to the right. The same principle applies.

Of course, if you're as strong as an Ian Woosnam, the 1991 Masters champion, you can overpower the design of many holes. The last hole at Augusta National is a dogleg right, with deep bunkers guarding the left side. Woosnam won by simply smashing a high, hard hook over the bunkers and out into an area the members use for practice. That's his natural shot, and he's comfortable with it. He had a short iron to the green, and made the par he needed.

It wasn't an impulsive move. Woosnam had tried driving the ball over the bunkers in practice rounds to make sure he could clear them safely. Also, the tee was moved up on the final day. I think that confused me and Jose Maria Olazabal, but it played right into Woosnam's strategy. He found a new way to play the hole, and eliminated all the trouble.

Trevino has always said that the 18th at Augusta is the one hole on the course that fits his fader's game. He goes to the right side of the tee—the correct side for him—and in effect straightens out the hole.

If you hit the ball from left to right, tee up on the right side of the teeing ground.

ALLOW PLENTY OF ROOM
FOR YOUR SHOT SHAPE

In all of this you have to remember to aim for your slice if you're a slicer, or for your hook if you're a hooker. Most golfers don't allow enough for the typical shape of their shots. If you slice the ball 35 yards, you may have to aim left of the fairway to get it in play.

Especially if the wind is blowing from the left. Not only will the ball blow to the right, it will land and then kick and roll more in that direction.

You don't have to tee off with a driver (many times it's smarter to go with a 3-wood or even an iron for more control). Consider that the longer the club, the more sidespin you will put on the ball and the more it will slice or hook. A long iron will curve much more than a short iron.

WHERE IS THE FLAG?

One of the things I make sure I know every time I stand up on the tee is where the flag is on the green. I ask my caddie where the flag is. Because if it's on the right side of the green and the tee shot is relatively straight, I want my drive to finish in the left side of the fairway.

You have more green to work with from the left side of the fairway. Especially if there is a bunker or water hazard to the right of the green, I have more room for error. If I mis-hit it a little bit from the left side of the fairway, the ball will still land on the green.

OTHER TEEING TRICKS

I tee the ball so half of it is above the top of my driver. I will tee it up a little bit lower going into the wind, a little bit higher going downwind. With a metal wood, tee the ball slightly lower, because the ball launches higher, I find.

You have the benefit of going back two club-lengths to tee it up in a tee box. You should use that length to your advantage. If you are a good enough player to understand that you are in between two clubs, a 5-iron and a 6-iron for example, those two club-lengths you're allowed can make a difference of going over the green or being short on a par 3. You can tee the ball so you have a good, full swing at the ball with the right club.

Sometimes off the tee with a driver or 3-wood, you don't want the most length. That's strategy. Maybe you want to stay short of the bunkers that pinch the fairway at 220 yards. Remember you have the option of hitting from a couple of club-lengths back. Or you might want to move back to get a level stance.

Beware of tee markers that are angled off line.

Smart teeing takes in a lot of tactics.

CHAPTER 5
How to Straighten Out Those Doglegs

Playing doglegs is like driving a car around a corner. You want the smoothest, most efficient route possible. In effect, you want to straighten out the dogleg. That begins with paying careful attention to where you tee the ball.

In the example illustrated on the next two pages, a sharp dogleg to the right, I move all the way to the left edge of the teeing ground. The rules allow me to stand outside the teeing ground as long as the ball is inside it.

From here the hole plays straighter. I have more fairway to work with, and if I hit my drive into the ideal position I may be able to hit two to three clubs less to the green. There always is a preferable side of the fairway on a dogleg. Hitting it will set up a shorter, simpler second shot.

Every summer I play a couple of rounds at the Greenbrier resort in West Virginia with a few friends who happen to represent a cross section of weekend golfers. The 11th hole, on the Old White Course there, is a 409-yard par 4 from the white markers that doglegs dramatically to the left about 175 yards out from the tee. Sand and trees lurk to the left, with plenty of room to the right.

The tee itself is probably 15 yards wide. Almost every one of my friends teed the ball on the left side of the tee and made the dogleg sharper until I told them to tee on the right side and lessen the effect of the dogleg. That way the hole plays straighter.

The length of the hole and the situation at the corner must be considered. If there's a lot of trouble at the corner of a dogleg par 4, and you'd have to hit your two best shots to get home, consider playing away from the corner. Play the par 4 as a par 5.

It helps to know where the flagstick is located on the green, especially on a shorter hole that doglegs abruptly. We have that luxury on the tour—our caddies are provided with diagrams—but you can discover a lot of hole locations in advance by checking greens you'll play later, when you pass them early in the round.

Which way does the ground slope in the landing area? Could it kick your ball into trouble? You have to know.

By moving as far left as I can to tee off, I turn this dogleg into a straighter hole.

How bad is the rough? If it's light enough, I might purposely drive into the rough to shorten the hole.

The main key to playing doglegs, though, is to give yourself the best angle off the tee. That's how you turn a crooked hole into a straight hole and simplify your assignment.

ALLOW FOR WIND AND SHOT SHAPE

What if you regularly slice or hook the ball? What if a crosswind is blowing on a dogleg?

If you hit the ball from left to right and the fairway moves from left to right (with no wind) you should feel comfortable. Favor the left side of the tee so you straighten the angle of the dogleg. (If the hole turns left, tee the ball on the right side.)

Now let's confront the wind. You're a left-to-right player on a left-to-right hole with a strong left-to-right wind. Tee the ball on the right side and aim away from the corner of the dogleg. Aim at the left rough, because the wind will magnify your slice and you'll wind up in the fairway. Conversely, if the wind is coming strongly from right to left, tee up on the left side and aim down the middle of the fairway. The wind will take the slice out of your shot.

Just adjust this thinking for right-to-left holes and shot shapes.

WHEN TO CUT THE CORNER

Know your nature. Are you aggressive or conservative? A good player has to know when to be aggressive and when to be conservative. Jack Nicklaus is an aggressive player but one who at times will play very conservatively.

The macho bit may be good for the Terminator, but it doesn't always work on the golf course. The weekend player needs to understand his own nature when faced with the many difficult decisions that must be made on doglegs. Understand the situation and your strengths and weaknesses.

Generally speaking, if you slice you should be aggressive on dogleg rights. If you hook, be aggressive on dogleg lefts. If the wind is helping you take a shortcut, so much the better. When the doglegs go in the other direction, be conservative.

Know the odds. It's like gambling in Las Vegas or Atlantic City. For pulling a shot off, I think low odds are 1 out of 2 and high odds 3-1. In match play you might gamble against much longer odds than these if your opponent has an advantage. (That's the beauty of match play.) In stroke play I usually cannot afford to run a big risk unless I'm in position to win a tournament and need to chance it near the end.

Know your yardages. When you hit across a dogleg, make certain you know your short-yardage and long-yardage limits. Many times you will face a dogleg of 60 to 90 degrees, and it's hard to bend the ball that much even if you are a good enough shotmaker.

This is a hook hole. If you are a slicer, where would you not want to drive the ball? Where is your negative-negative? The right trees. Even if you drive it in there and have a clear shot, a bunker guards the front-right part of the green and the pin. The front right of the green is lower than the back left. My positive-negative miss off the tee would be to the left side in the fairway bunkers. From there, you can advance the ball up in front of the green or you might even be

A. Ravielli

able to blade the ball out of the bunker and roll it up the left side of the green, since there's no bunker guarding the green over there. The best drive, my positive-positive, is up the right side of the fairway. With this pin position you have a better slope to hit your approach into. If you carry it long, the ball is going to stop. You have a backstop. A slicer has to aim the drive at the bunkers or left of the bunkers and let the ball curve back into the fairway. You have to trust your slice.

Colonial Country Club in Fort Worth has a lot of sharp doglegs like that—the 436-yard 15th hole you see on television for instance. It turns right around bunkers and trees at the corner. That's a true shot-maker's course.

Determine the distance you have to hit the ball to carry the near edge of the rough but not roll through the fairway into the far rough. In other words create a complete target picture, with boundaries short, long, left and right. Again, it's like driving a car around a corner.

CHAPTER 6
Attacking Par-3, Par-4 and Par-5 Holes

To think your way strategically around the golf course, you have to understand what the architect had in mind when he designed it. I've never heard so much debate over course design as I've been listening to lately. It seems every golfer has a a sharp opinion about every hole he plays. Talking about golf design is as subjective as arguing over modern art or the best barbecue sauce in the world (I am something of an authority on the latter), which is one reason it's so much fun for all of us.

I favor holes that are essentially strategic. By that I mean they have built-in safety features. My main complaint with modern architecture is that there are not enough places to bail out. A hole should have a risky side and a safe side, which can vary with the flagstick positions. The greater the risk, the greater the potential reward—but you ought to have a choice. You should be able to play safely and take a long route, or take the risk and play the shortcut.

As a tour pro, I can live with having to hit one extremely demanding shot after another, but it's not enjoyable, and golf should be enjoyable at any level of play. If the weather turns poor, you have an impossible task. A good player should have to hit two or three perfect shots a round—not nine or 10. When I hear people boasting that their course has water in play on 15 holes, I wonder if they own the ball concession. Get a 30-mile-per-hour wind and you have to close the place down.

I also like some greens to be open in front and elevated a bit. Many architects today will not do greens that way. Heaven forbid we should see one on a TPC course! One of the most strategic and historic design concepts in golf is being lost.

IT'S A MIND GAME

The other day in the locker room somebody said that golf is 90 percent mental. "Yeah," piped up somebody else, "and 65 percent physical." I don't know the exact breakdown, but I know you have to think well to play well, and I know weekend players underestimate the importance of

Par 4

Par 5

Par 3

Knowing where to miss is crucial to playing any length hole.

tactics. Once you've learned to strike the ball acceptably, strategy influences your scoring tremendously.

As I said earlier, I stress three dimensions when I talk about strategy: You have to understand your personal capabilities, you have to understand the trouble spots on the course, and you have to play every shot with the next shot in mind. Combine these three elements and you will become a smart golfer.

WHERE CAN YOU RECOVER FROM?

Understand the wind, too. If the wind is blowing hard from right to left on the hole, it is awfully hard to come in from the right side of the green when the pin is on the right. I want to be on the left side for my approach so I have more green to work with, because the wind will move the ball left. You have more green to land the ball and have it roll up to the hole when you are in the left side of the fairway and the pin is on the right. And vice versa when the pin is on the left. This is strategy.

If you are a slicer and the pin is on the left side of the green, you have a tougher shot. Try to play the ball to the right side of the fairway given a straight fairway. Then you can hit the ball more to the left side of the green and have more green to work with.

Sometimes you even have to aim the ball left of the green. Let the wind and the natural curve of your shot bring it in.

Most people want to aim straight at the hole, but the ball curves in the air if you slice it or hook it and you have to play for that. And you have to understand how much the wind will push it—or hold it up.

Then you have to evaluate the trouble near your target. Where can you miss your approach and still get up and down? If the flag's left and there's a deep bunker left, but you can chip and putt from the right side, you don't want to miss left. That's tactics.

Let's look at holes of different lengths and types, applying these principles. I'll give you some famous holes as examples.

There are enough different ways to play different holes to fill a library. A hole never plays the same twice, due to the wind if nothing else. That is a great part of golf's joy. But the following examples will give you a good grounding.

Enjoy the game by playing the tees that make the most sense for you. If you can't carry the ball 200 yards, stay away from the back tees. It's a whole different strategy back there.

HOW TO PLAY PAR 3s

If you are an average player or high handicapper on my team in a pro-am, I want you to help on the par-3 holes. You should make more pars on the 3s than on the par 4s and par 5s, simply because the 3s are shorter. You have to hit only one good shot and you can see from the tee how it sets up.

Unfortunately, too many bogeys, double bogeys and worse are made on the easiest holes because golfers don't plan them carefully enough. You may fail to consider that the architect often makes up for the lack of distance on a par 3 by designing more trouble into it.

It sounds odd, but tour pros have more trouble with par 3s because we hit the ball farther than you do. I'm a long hitter, and on many courses I will be using short irons for my approach shots until I come to a par 3—when suddenly I need a middle iron or long iron from the back tees. I may not have hit a middle iron or long iron all day.

Here's an axiom I think will help you make more pars and birdies on the par 3s, where you should make them. Apply it rigorously and I'll want you on my side in a pro-am.

SAFE PART VS. FAT PART

Distinguish between the safe part of the green and the fat part. Play for the safe part, not the fat part. I wish I had a new golf ball for every time I've heard that you should hit to the fat part of the green. The fat part and the safe part might be the same, but frequently they are not. Go for the area where there's the least trouble. The safe area may even include a portion of the fringe or fairway.

I've played a lot of par 3s where this axiom holds. The sixth at Augusta National is one. The fat part of the green—in this case the left side—is severely humped and protected by heavy bunkering. If you hit the green on that side, you face a roller-coaster putt. If you miss this fat side, you're probably in a deep bunker. The safe part of the green—the right side—is smaller, but it's flat and free of trouble. Even if you miss the green to the right you will have a simple, uphill putt or chip.

Occasionally you have no way to play safely. The 11th hole at Shinnecock Hills on Long Island, the site of the centennial U.S. Open in 1995, plays to an elevated green surrounded by deep bunkers and rough. You must hit the green. There's no bailout.

The 17th hole at the famous Taheiyo Club in Japan, where I've played tournaments, is a tremendously challenging par 3. It's about 190 yards downhill to a green with a big hogback running up the center. The green slopes to either side from the center and down in front. You have to carry the front bunkers.

The toughest shot on a par 3 is when the flagstick is short, just over a bunker. You don't want to be long and face a fast putt down the slope—but you don't want to be short and possibly bury the ball in the bunker. You simply must hit a fine shot.

A par 3 doesn't need to be long to be arduous. The seventh hole at Pebble Beach is only 107 yards—and it's downhill. But it can be a little monster.

With no wind, this is a straightforward pitch shot to a tiny green sur-

DOWNHILL

-1 Club

UPHILL

+1 Club

Play for the safe part of the green, even though it isn't as large. On uphill and downhill par 3s, add or subtract a club for about every 30 feet of elevation.

rounded by bunkers with Carmel Bay behind. But into the wind it's one of the most frightening holes in golf. One year in the Bing Crosby—I mean the AT&T—I hit two 5-irons and a 6-iron the three days we played it! One year when the wind was really howling in off the water, Sam Snead actually putted the ball down the hill and into a bunker.

The 17th at Harbour Town is a wonderful par 3 that I have played with anything from a 9-iron to a 2-iron depending on the wind. The green is very narrow with water left and front. A bunker also left has a unique hazard: If you hit the ball too far off line you could have your backswing restricted by an infamous Pete Dye railroad tie. To the right of the green are a bunker and a little swale. Your bailout area is right and long. For slicers, it's a good option. Take more club and carry the bunker on the right. If the flag is middle or back, you'll have an easy, flat chip shot.

The key feature of the hole is the narrowness of the green. It's in the shape of a banana basically. Any flag on the green is a tough position. It's an easy green to putt but a most difficult green to hit. You simply must produce a good shot.

Sometimes the hole presents no option. But usually there's a safe way out if you study the hole. Always consider your alternatives.

I'll never forget playing with Jack Nicklaus some years ago when he beat me in the Hawaiian Open. I had a chance to catch him coming to the 17th hole, a long, dangerous par 3 that was easy to double-bogey.

Jack wasn't playing very well the last day. The flag was back left, near a difficult bunker. He played to the safer right-front of the green with a short club, a 6-iron, and two-putted from 50 feet for his par to kill my chances. He made sure he couldn't make a double bogey. That taught me a valuable lesson strategically.

Your chances of two-putting for par from anywhere will be good on most par-3 greens because these greens tend to be smaller.

ALWAYS TEE IT UP

Always tee the ball on a par 3. I see too many people being macho and carelessly throwing the ball on the grass. They hit a flyer or worse. When hitting the ball off grass, I'm not able to tell consistently what it will do.

I tee the ball a little higher than grass level. The oval part of the tee, but none of the stem, is showing. For a longer club I'll tee it a little higher. Then I just hit the ball in the back.

Avoid the tendency to swing up on the ball because it's on a tee. A good thought is to try to break the tee on a par 3. Don't flick at it. Stay down with the shot and keep the clubhead on your target line going through the ball, just as if the ball were on grass.

TAKE AN EXTRA CLUB

Playing par-3 holes, the emphasis should be on tactics rather than power. Club selection is crucial. Most weekend golfers don't hit enough club on par 3s. Maybe you don't want to hit more club than your playing partners...or you don't notice that the green is elevated...or you don't appreciate that the worst trouble is in front of the green.

A good rule of thumb is to take one more club than you think you need. Or try to land the ball on top of the flagstick. That will help you pick enough club. When in doubt, take the longer club.

STAYING SHORT CAN BE SMART

Don't be too proud to lay up on the long par 3 you cannot reach comfortably. When Billy Casper won the 1959 U.S. Open at Winged Foot, he laid up all four days at the treacherous third hole, which played at 200 yards plus. The narrow green is open in front but is pinched by deep bunkers on both sides. Not far behind the green is out-of-bounds. Hit your tee ball above the hole and you probably will three-putt.

Casper knew that his odds of making par for four days were much better laying up, and he was taking double bogey out of the picture. Also by laying up he could hit a shorter club and pick up accuracy. He made par every day. That's a consummate example of thinking-man's golf. He knew the hole, knew his capabilities and knew he would gain strokes on the field by resisting any macho tendencies he might feel.

Players who don't hesitate to lay up on a long, tricky par 4 and par 5 don't seem able to do it on a par 3 they can seldom, if ever, reach. Lay up so you have a chance to get close on your second shot and you'll make a lot more pars than you will by gambling with your tee shot, especially if you're a better than average chipper and putter. And you'll avoid a terrible score. Forget par, which realistically may be 4 for you on a difficult par 3.

Look on par 3s as a test in tactics. Think your way to pars and birdies. Practicing on a par-3 course or executive course is a good way to lower your scores.

ADJUST CLUB SELECTION FOR ELEVATION

On uphill and downhill par 3s, add or subtract a club for about every 30 feet of elevation. The difference in elevation usually is greater on downhill shots, which means the wind can be a major factor because the ball stays in the air so long. But uphill shots are tougher because the ball comes in on a flatter trajectory and the ball won't stop as soon.

HOW TO PLAY SHORT PAR 4s

There is no average length for a par 4. The U.S. Golf Association's range runs from 251 yards to 470 yards. When you factor in elevation and wind, the bracket can get even broader. I've driven a par 4 in Japan that's 360 yards—but the tee shot is downwind and the tee is 50 feet above the fairway.

On a short par 4, I plot the hole from the flag back. Where is the flag on the green? That tells me which side of the fairway I want to drive to, or even what part of the rough I want to be in if I'll have a better angle from the rough than the fairway. If the flag is on the right side of the green, I want to be going at it from the left side of the fairway or the left rough.

Or if I'm debating whether to try to drive the green, the position of the flag is crucial. I applaud the revived thinking in course design to include at least one challenging little par 4 that you can drive if you want to run a formidable risk. You can drive the ball on the green, but the penalty for missing may be severe—you might make a 6 or worse.

Usually I don't try to drive the green unless the wind is behind me and I have a fairly inviting target area, or I'm playing match play and the situation dictates running the risk. If the flag is in the front of the green and the wind is behind me, I usually want to lay back off the tee so I can hit a full sand wedge for my second shot and put a lot of backspin on the ball to make it stop. If I drive the ball 40 yards short of the green, I'll have a much more difficult wedge shot that I won't be able to stop near the hole.

Is the risk of going for the green worth the reward? Do you need to make a birdie on the hole? If you miss your drive, where are you likely to wind up? How much trouble will you be in? You should try to eliminate penal hazards like water or out-of-bounds, especially in medal play. If the driver can get you in dire trouble, maybe you want to play a 4-iron to a safe landing area. You still will have just a short iron for your second shot.

Playing for position with your tee shot on a short par 4 is like playing a par-3 tee shot. You want to set up the best angle for your next shot. Stay away from bad trouble and give yourself a chance to attack with your second shot.

The temptation on a short par 4 is to want to drive the ball close to the green. Often there is a grave risk in that. You will flirt with hazards or leave yourself with a difficult little approach.

The sixth hole at Winged Foot's West Course is a great example of a short par 4 where any player needs to play for position because the risks of gambling are too great. It's only 324 yards, the shortest par 4 on the course, but it's extremely demanding. It gives you options.

You cannot drive the ball to the right, even the right side of the fair-

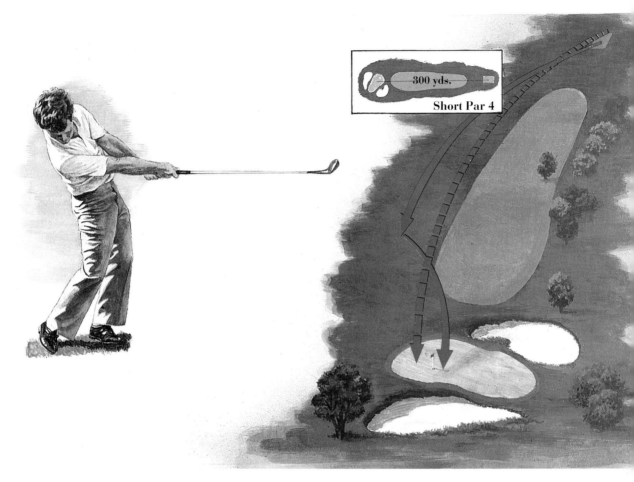

300 yds.

Short Par 4

I might try to drive the green on this 300-yard par 4 if the wind's behind me, because the flag's in an attackable position. The best lay up would be a middle iron into the light rough, to my right, then a full short iron up the length of the green, avoiding the deep bunkers. Either way I'm eliminating the left half of the hole—it's much tougher.

way. Large trees hug the right side, and at best your angle to the green will be lousy. You'll have to come in over a fearsome bunker to the shallow part of the green, and if you go long on that line you can be in a creek.

You must play the hole up the left side the whole way. You have extra room over there plus a good angle into the green. There's a fairly easy bunker about 260 yards out on the left side, and most of you wouldn't be able to reach it with a driver. If you think you could, or you aren't hitting your driver straight, hit your 3-wood, which will leave you an 8-iron or 9-iron. I probably will hit a 3-wood and a wedge.

If you are a slicer, tee it up near the right marker and aim over in the left rough. Teeing up on the left would encourage a result that is too far right. Aim at the left rough and the ball will bend into the left side of the fairway, which is ideal. Actually, the left rough gives you the best angle into the green. It's a straight hole, but a slicer needs to play it as a left-to-right dogleg. Otherwise you'll have no shot home.

From the left side, or the left rough, I will hit for the opening at the left front of the green. If the ball bounces well, it will get up where I'll have a putt for birdie. If it doesn't, I'm still in good shape for a par. You can make par there with smart play even if you're an 18-handicapper.

The ninth hole at Cypress Point in California is shorter—less than 300 yards from the back tees—but much harder for the average player to par. I've seen a lot of 7s and 8s and pickups there. I can drive the ball on the green under favorable conditions, but the penalty for missing is extreme.

It's a dunesy hole. The fairway narrows sharply at about 190 yards out, and you have to be very accurate to hit the little neck there off the tee. That's the main challenge for the average player.

The green is shallow and very low on the right front where there's an entrance through which you can run the ball. The rest of the green is protected by dunes bunkering. Less than half the green is pinnable because of a big slope in the middle.

Your options are to drive the ball as close to the green as you can and then play a wedge to the green, or play safely with a middle iron off the tee and a short-iron lay up toward the opening on the right of the green, and hope to chip and putt for a par. (A middle-iron approach won't hold the green.) If the flag is on the right and you play safely, your chances for par will be good. If it's on the left, a bogey is likely. But you won't be making an awful score.

It's vital to know your distances when you're analyzing a hole this way. At least on your home course you should know them.

I've played this hole different ways. One is to hit a fairway wood up within 50 yards of the green, then hit a flip wedge. I usually drive up the right side because the flag is usually left. The flip wedge is not a good option downwind, particularly if the flag is back left, because it's too hard to hold the green. It's definitely not a good option if you don't handle the shot well.

The best option for me with a strong wind behind me, although a dangerous one, is to try to drive the green. It's the kind of option Tom Kite exercised on the par-5 14th hole the final day when he won the 1992 U.S. Open. He hit a splendid drive and rejected the option of hitting a middle-iron lay up and then a full wedge with a lot of spin. He knew he couldn't hold that green downwind even with a well-struck wedge, so he went for the green and got close enough for a relatively simple short shot that led to a birdie. The problem on the ninth at Cypress is that you're driving into a tight area, and if you hit it crookedly you may well be blasting out of trouble sideways.

Another way I can play that hole is with a middle iron off the tee to give myself a full short iron into the green. But I still have to hit a nearly perfect second shot. The hole can eat your lunch.

The eighth at Pine Valley is a great short par 4. I'll use it to demonstrate how you sometimes want to use radical, "cowardly" strategy to play around your weaknesses and score better.

It's 310 yards, and the drive kicks downhill. The tee shot is blind, with the fairway opening up generously to the right (a second alternate green has been built to the right of the old one, but I'm assuming here we're playing the old one). The green is extremely narrow, with penal traps cut up into it on both sides. The second shot is absolutely pivotal.

The right side of the fairway is the easiest to drive to, particularly for a slicer, but the left side is preferable because from there you can shoot up the length of the green. From the right side you have to come in across a severe bunker and land the ball on a sliver of green with another severe bunker on the far side. I've seen people go back and forth from one of those bunkers to the other like a Ping-Pong match.

The green is elevated and three tiered. Going over the green is better than being wide. There's no sand and you can play from over the green, even though the ball will be going down the slope of the green coming back.

I hit a 3-wood and a wedge. The second is a must-play shot. You may have a downhill stance to a small, uphill target. I never flirt with the edges of that green. It isn't worth it. I'll play for the middle, and if I get the distance right I'll have a good birdie chance.

You might argue that it's too penal a hole, and there's been a lot of talk about softening it. But I think every course should have a must-play shot. Not more than one or two, though—too many new courses are being built with six or seven, and that takes the fun out of the game for any of us.

If you would have to hit your best shot to put the ball on this green and you aren't a reliable sand player, I'd recommend that you go so far, or so near, as to hit a wedge 30 or 40 yards, short of the green and the bunkers, and then hit another short shot through the opening to the green. Put the ball in front of the green, not in the sand.

Let's say you have a stroke on the hole and hit a good drive. Lay up short to the left, then pitch the ball up the angle of the green. Unless you're a slicer. If you're a slicer and you're in the right side of the fairway, the natural curve of your approach shot will be going up the length of the green, a plus. But if you have a longish iron, or you're a hooker, forget about hitting that narrow green. You'll get in bad trouble much more often than not, and you may not be able to finish the hole.

Short par 4s can present grand opportunities—and grand challenges. Don't let the lack of yardage make you too greedy.

HOW TO PLAY MEDIUM PAR 4s

To me a medium-length par 4 is one you can reach in two without straining under normal conditions—but may not always want to try to reach if you're an average player. You have to weigh your risk/reward factor carefully on your approach shot if there's serious trouble near the green as there often is on this length hole.

Where is the trouble? Where is the flag? Where is the wind?

If the flag is in the back part of the green and there's a big bunker in front, missing your approach into that bunker and having to play a long sand shot is not a good prospect for most of you. You'd be better off laying up short of the bunker and pitching the ball up to the hole, especially if it's one of your stroke holes.

The wind is a key factor. If the hole is 365 yards but it's into a wind that's blowing 30 miles an hour in your face, you may not be able to reach the green anyway. So why take a chance against long odds? Lay up to good position for a chip or pitch.

The first hole at Augusta National lists at 365 yards from the member tees but plays much longer because it's steeply uphill. The hole is much easier if you can carry the gaping fairway bunker on the right. Most of the pros can nowadays. It's a 250-yard carry for us, and I stress the word carry. You have to fly the ball all that way, sometimes against the wind. For the members it's a 210-yard carry over the bunker.

The approach is simpler from the right side of the fairway because you can avoid the bunker at the left front of the green with your second shot. Don't do what Marty Fleckman did in his first Masters, though. He swung extra hard on the tee trying to clear the bunker, and drove the ball so far right he cleared the main leader board, just missed the press building and lost his ball. Nobody can remember a ball going that far right on the hole.

The safe route is to stay well left of the fairway bunker. You'll have a less appealing second shot, but the hole's a hard par anyway. If you make a good chip and putt from the opening on the right of the green, you can make par and probably no worse than bogey, especially if the flag's on the

Medium Par 4

365 yds.

If trouble menaces your drive and approach shot on a medium par 4 into the wind, you probably should lay up. Especially consider laying up if you get a handicap stroke. Play up the safe side of the hole all the way.

front right. If you lay up on your approach, lay up to the right. You'll be behind mounds, but you can deal with them easier than that left bunker.

Your strategy may depend on how confident you feel on the first tee. Do you want to attempt a long carry with your opening drive?

It's a very underrated hole. The tour pros are never unhappy with a par score there.

The 12th at Harbour Town is another good medium-length par 4 on the tour. It has a unique green, and you must, must plot the hole from the flag back to the tee. The green is in two separate sections—the back left is offset from the front right. A bunker fronts the back-left part and borders the front-right part. Another bunker is on the outside of the front-right section.

Your approach will be either to the back left or front right, and there can be a three-club difference. Both parts of the green are quite small. Over the green to the right is a low area that's not a bad place to miss the ball. You need to know that before you play the hole.

It's a dogleg right, with trees up both sides. If the flag is front right, you ideally drive the ball into the right center of the fairway (if you're a slicer, your shot shape can help you if you aim far enough left). If you go too far right, the overhanging trees will block your shot to the pin. Make sure you don't miss it right when the flag's right. Your safety drive is left, which leaves you a longer approach and a more awkward angle. Even the left rough is OK when the flag's front right.

If the flag is back left, your options are more limited. The best drive is center of the fairway. Go too far left and you're in the trees. Go too far right and you have a longer shot to a tiny green area guarded by sand.

I hope the trees on Harbour Town stop growing soon.

No. 8 at Riviera in the Los Angeles area is one of the best medium par 4s I've played. It's only 368 yards, but it can sucker-punch you if you aren't careful. It's a dogleg right with trees up the entire right side and a fairway bunker left off the tee. Laying up short of the bunker is the safer route, but it leaves you a longer shot to a challenging green.

The narrow green is sort of a dogleg left. There's an upslope into the right side of the green and a downslope off the left back. You feel you can make birdie when the flag's on the right side, but you are happy with par when the flag's on the left.

If you're a big hitter, you can hit the ball over the fairway bunker. I've heard that Ben Hogan would lay up short of the bunker with a 3-iron, then hit a 5-iron approach. He could control a 5-iron well enough to go at that left flag position. But it's too easy to misjudge your distance just slightly and come up short or long. If you're short, you have to chip over a mound and stop the ball on the downslope. It's better to be long, but then you're over the green. And that Kikuyu grass grabs the ball around the green.

The best place to be, especially going at the left flag position, is in the right side of the fairway—but that's the dangerous route because of the overhanging trees. I will hit driver (unless the hole is playing downwind) and try to slide the ball off the right edge of the fairway bunker.

With the flag back left, I want to be hitting a wedge from the right side of the fairway into the middle of the green, drawing it slightly from right to left so it lands and spins left. If the flag is on the right, with the ground sloping up to it, it's better to be short than long.

There's a hole that will ask you to cut the ball off the tee and draw it into the green. It's a shotmaker's hole.

The 13th hole at Phoenix Country Club in Japan, where there's a big tournament every fall, is a 90-degree dogleg left, 360 yards, and I try to be as precise as possible with my driving distance. Again the flag dictates my strategy.

If the flag is left, I want to hit the ball farther off the tee because there's room to drive it up through the dogleg to get a better angle in. Even if I go through the fairway 10 yards, I'll have a clear shot at the flag. If the flag's right, I'll lay back off the tee to go at the flag. That influences my club selection on the tee. With no wind, a 3-wood will be my long club and a 1-iron my short club.

You can't see the flag from the tee, so it's essential to find out where it is before you play the hole.

HOW TO PLAY LONG PAR 4s

Once a hole gets up around 400 yards it plays like a par 5 for most amateurs. It's a three-shot hole unless it's downwind or downhill or both. If you'd have to crank out a good drive and good 3-wood to get home, the odds of making par are not favorable. Get a downhill lie for the 3-wood and they are worse. You'd have a better chance hitting three iron shots you can control.

Let's say the hole is 430 yards. You can hit a 5-iron 150 yards off the tee, advance another 5-iron 150 yards and hit an 8-iron 130 onto the green. You don't have to force any of those shots. If you hit your 5-iron 160 yards rather than 150, you'll be hitting a wedge to the green.

This conservative strategy usually has the added benefit of keeping you away from the major trouble on the hole. You'll be short of it on the first two shots and probably will be playing a fairly undemanding third shot to a large flattish green when the hole's this long. You won't make worse than bogey very often, and you'll eliminate the high number you could make going for the green with two long shots.

Use what Bob Murphy calls "positive-negative" thinking. Ask yourself first where you can't afford to miss the ball...where is the trouble to avoid. If trees hang over the right side of the fairway, stay away from the right side. Aim for the left side, which is clear. Do this on each shot.

Some players can't play safely. They think they'd be showing a lack of courage. Maybe they enjoy the game more taking unreasonable chances, but if you want to lower your handicap this year, the way to do it is to play more strategically, more consistently.

If you cannot reach a long par 4 without hitting two of your best wood shots, forget about going for it. Play three conservative shots so you never flirt with trouble.

430 yds.

Long Par 4

The fifth at Augusta National is a long, strong par 4 hardly anyone sees because it's the farthest hole from the clubhouse. It's a dogleg left, 435 yards from the tournament tees and 405 from the member tees. It looks like a wide-open driving hole, and it is if you don't mind lengthening your second shot by hitting out to the right. Sand and trees are left—that's the shorter, riskier line. Ian Woosnam duck-hooked his drive over there in 1992 and had to go back to the tee. He gambled and lost.

If I drive it up the left side I might have as little as an 8-iron to the green, and I'll be shooting straight up the slope of the green. The green is tricky—it comes to a point in the middle, and the ball can take off either way when it lands. From the left side you can keep the ball on the green fairly easily, but from the right side it's hard to do. My trade-off for hitting a simple tee shot is I'm hitting a long iron to the green from an oblique angle and almost have to run the ball on. The ball will back off the green as readily as not.

If you are playing the hole and don't want it to take you to task, the safe tack is to drive the ball to the right, avoiding the bunkers and woods. Then, lay up your second shot to the right and run the ball up the slope to the hole from there. Bob Kletcke, the Augusta club pro, sums it up: The farther right you go, the wider the target.

The eighth hole at Winged Foot West is 442 yards from the championship tees and 427 from the regular tees. It's the No. 1 handicap hole, with good reason. It's a long, grueling, dogleg right with a blind tee shot. Big trees menace the drive on the right, little pine trees keep growing on the left. You are tempted to aim your tee shot at a big green water tower in the left background, but there isn't as much room that way as you think. Those little pines will stymie you.

If you're a slicer, you might want to hit the driver there. Even if you put it in the right rough you can get a good look at the green. Otherwise, if you have trouble cutting the ball, you probably are better off laying up with a fairway wood off the tee.

In either case, if you can't drive the ball well over 200 yards, you are better off laying up. And if you're going to lay up, why put pressure on any shot, including the tee shot? It's a stroke hole. Would you be satisfied to be in the fairway about 100 yards from the green for your third shot? If you would, why not hit two 170-yard shots to get there? Put your drive in play 170 yards, then hit your second shot another 170 and you've left yourself a 100-yard wedge shot to the green. You've taken the risk out of the hardest hole on the golf course and set yourself up for a short approach and a one-putt par.

Don't stop thinking now, though. The green slopes off quickly to the right, and if the flag's on the right side don't fool with it. You can't stop the ball on the green.

HOW TO PLAY PAR 5s

Par-5 holes are the easiest for a professional to play—but the toughest for the average golfer. It's mainly a matter of sheer length. My three shots on a par 5 might vary 300 yards in distance from your three shots.

A strong player can make up for a poor shot on a par 5 with a good long shot and at least save par, if not make birdie. A weekend player needs to put three good shots together even though he often has trouble putting one good shot together. The longer the hole, the more chances he has to foul up.

That's the negative news. The good news is that you can save more strokes on par-5 holes than anywhere else on the golf course if you use sensible, realistic tactics.

And when you put together a couple of quality shots, you will have a chance for a birdie. Par 5s are the opportune birdie holes.

Don't let the yardage on the scorecard intimidate you on a par 5. Analyze the hole by sections, starting from the flagstick whenever possible and plotting your strategy in reverse. Walk the par 5s on your home course backward to understand their design (pick a quiet time to do this). This is the way I'd like you to think:

THIRD SHOT. How far do you want to be from the green for your approach? (Maybe it's your fourth shot.) I don't want to be 40 yards out with a wedge in my hand, especially if the wind is behind me and the pin's up front. That's too tricky a shot. I make more birdies when I have a full wedge or even a longer club to the green, because I can hit the ball hard and put backspin on it to make it stop.

Whatever the club, be sure it's enough to get you over the trouble that architects like to put in front of a par-5 green to threaten big hitters going for it in two. You have to carry that minefield or risk severe penalties. Know how far you carry the ball with your different clubs.

SECOND SHOT. It can be deceptively dangerous. Too many people assume they have to hit it a long way and get as close to the green as possible, if not reach the green. But how many times do you see a weekend golfer top his second shot with a fairway wood—often from a lie that would discourage a pro from hitting a wood? If you have a poor lie, forget about hitting a long shot, let alone going for the green.

It could make more sense for you to lay up with a middle iron and open up the green for your third shot. Remember it's a game of angles, and you want to be able to attack the pin with your third shot, playing into as much green as possible.

Keep in mind that a par 5 is supposed to be designed as a three-shot hole and almost always will be a three-shotter for the average player. Two putts give you par, a good score. It won't show on the scorecard what clubs you hit for those three shots. If you hit your typical 5-iron about 160 yards, and the hole is 480, you can play three 5-iron shots and reach the green in regulation!

I might well use a driver and 4-wood when the hole is comfortably reachable and the hazards are easy to clear. I emphasize the word comfort-

Plot par-5 strategy in reverse.

ably, and I'm assuming a good lie for the fairway shot. You perhaps should hit a 3-wood, 5-iron and 8-iron.

TEE SHOT. Resist the natural urge to crush the ball because it's a long hole. The harder you swing, the more chance you have to miss the shot and spoil the hole immediately. Think position instead of power. Where do you want to go to set up your second shot? Aim and align yourself carefully.

Consider using a 3-wood or even less club off the tee. The key is to drive the ball safely in play. You can reach the green with your next two shots, or three if necessary. Be conservative and don't press. What you absolutely don't want to do is drive into a bunker or the trees and forfeit any hope of a birdie or par. Focus on a target even if it's a wide fairway.

Almost every par 5 has a wide side and a narrow side. Drive into the

Here's how I might play the hole against a middle handicapper, if I were feeling strong.

safer outside lane and stay away from the trouble on the short side. Even if you defy the odds and hit the fairway on the narrow side, you probably will face a more difficult second shot. Play the angles.

WHEN TO GO FOR THE GREEN IN TWO

A lot of it for me depends on how I'm hitting the particular club the second shot calls for and the required shot shape. If the shot is a 1-iron with a fade, and I haven't been hitting that shot well lately, I'm going to lay up. The confidence factor is important.

Is the wind helping or hurting? That could be the decisive variable.

I will study whether there's an easy recovery side around the green if I mis-hit the shot. Can I keep alive a chance for birdie or even par if I go right of the green or left? Usually one side will be easier than the other. If you miss, miss to that side.

Finally, my position in the tournament is a consideration. Do I feel I need to go for it to win? If I do, I probably will run a greater risk. That can be high drama, but usually it's blown out of proportion. I can still make birdie by laying up and pitching and putting well.

The 18th hole at the Phoenix Country Club in Japan is a splendid, 535-yard par 5 that I almost never will try to reach in two. It's a narrow, treelined dogleg right, and the green is tightly guarded by deep sand and grass bunkers.

When I won there in 1980, I teed off with an iron into the wind. I knew I couldn't reach the green in two, so I took the trouble out of play.

Positioning of the second shot is critical. If the flag is in the left part of the green, you have to lay up to the right or vice versa. The best move is to lay up at least 80 yards short of the green. Otherwise you challenge the hole's narrowness. And, again, you want to hit a full wedge shot in.

The 18th hole at Pebble Beach is another terrific par 5 that I rarely try to reach in two. The ocean is in play from tee to green on the left, and there's out-of-bounds right. Positioning must be paramount in your mind.

I won our Open there in 1982 and drove with a 3-wood the last day, aiming right and drawing the ball. I laid up with a 7-iron to be short of the narrow part of the fairway. I wanted to leave myself a full 9-iron to the green because I'd hit a couple of mediocre partial-wedge shots that day. I made a nice, crisp swing with the 9-iron. The ball finished about 20 feet past the hole, and I made the birdie putt.

The 14th hole at Spanish Bay, a course I helped design on the Monterey Peninsula, makes you plot every shot thoughtfully. It's 571 yards from the back tees, 535 from the middle and 475 from the front, but it flows downhill toward the ocean the entire way and the fairway is generously wide.

I prefer to play the hole up the left side, because you ultimately can get at the green more easily. There's out-of-bounds off the tee, but large mounds to the left will kick the ball back toward the fairway. Also a quartering wind blows from left to right.

A huge bunker divides the broad fairway in the landing area for the second shot. The risky play is to hit your second shot up the narrow left side and thread the dunes and nasty little sod-faced bunkers. You'll be rewarded with an easy shot to the long green. The bailout on the second shot is to the right, but you leave yourself a longer third shot that will have to go over a marsh to a green that falls away from you on that line.

You can play short of that big fairway bunker with your second shot, but if you're too far short you'll have a semi-blind third shot with that marsh crowding in on the right. The second shot is the real key to the hole. It's a hole that makes you examine your risk/reward options on all three shots. If the wind turns against you, you have more of a test than you want. I've reached the green in two, but it's rarely the right idea.

The 12th at Oakmont you never can reach. I've reached it once—in a practice round. It stretches 603 yards with trouble the whole way. The fairway undulates and slants dangerously to the right in the driving zone, toward traps, rough and ditches, not to mention a downhill lie for your fairway-wood second shot. At best I'll have a wedge for my third shot to a swift green that's a snap to three-putt.

Many times I don't hit driver here because it's intimidatingly narrow between the bunkers left and right. At the 1983 U.S. Open at Oakmont, I hurt my chances by trying to hit a driver so I could get up there to hit an iron second shot and a wedge to the green. It was bad strategy. I should have hit 3-wood off the tee, safely short of the bunkers and in the fairway on a level lie. Instead I hit my driver well, but pulled it slightly into the left bunker.

I made a bogey and Larry Nelson wound up beating me in a playoff.

I've teed off with irons in some cases like this. You do it at Muirfield in Scotland to stay short of the very penal fairway bunkers. Those bunkers are like little water hazards.

Play for position on the par 5s. Whatever you do, stay well away from the hazards. Think a shot ahead and be strategic with your club selection. You'll make many more pars and birdies.

CHAPTER 7
Lay Up Like a Pool Player

Laying up intelligently means planning ahead and playing the angles. Think the way a good pool player does when he's setting up a run.

A recurring theme as we've talked about playing different kinds of holes has been the unsung practice of laying up if the odds are against you. Laying up can be smart on par-3, par-4 and par-5 holes, especially par 5s. But laying up has a stigma attached to it. You are not trying to hit your strongest shot; you are hitting a shorter, safer shot to get in position to hit a high-percentage shot.

Laying up to a pro is a science. More thought goes into it than you could ever guess watching television. Laying up is like playing pool. You always want to know where the cue ball is going to end up. You're always trying to make the shot at hand, but you also want to leave the cue ball in position to make the next shot. Good pool players are thinking not only one shot ahead but several shots ahead. That's how you make a run. The essence of laying up in golf is the same: Plan ahead to leave yourself in good position for the next shot, whether you're laying up short of trouble off the tee or on your subsequent shots on up to the green.

I don't use a go/no-go point on a hole. I've gone for a green from 250 yards out and laid up from 200, depending on my lie, the wind, how I stand in the tournament and how I feel at the time...particularly how I feel.

Several years ago I came to the final hole of the Taiheiyo Masters in Japan, a par 5 with a long water carry to the green. I needed a birdie to tie. I hit a good drive, and now I had a huge decision to make. I had 224 yards to carry the water and 240 to the flag. I laid up. Then I sculled my third shot over the green. I got up and down for par, but lost the tournament by a stroke.

Now I look like a fool and everybody is wondering why Watson laid up. Well, I took into account three factors. First, I wasn't hitting my 3-wood well that day. Second, the wind was in my face. Third, the ball was in a cuppy, skinny lie. I was not confident about my odds of bringing off the shot and by laying up I still had a chance to hit my third shot close and sink a birdie putt.

I didn't get my third shot close, but I almost certainly wouldn't have made par if I'd gone for the green in two. It was a psychological decision as much as anything else. I think I made the right decision even though I didn't get the desired result.

WHAT'S A SAFE CARRY?

For most players I think a safe carry is a 5-iron. If you have a good lie, with a cushion under the ball, then maybe you can hit a fairway wood. But if you have a tight lie it's too hard to get the ball up for a long carry. Late in Sam Snead's career, he said he was scoring better on par 5s because he'd stopped attempting any carry that required more than a comfortable iron shot.

Once in a while I'll try a risky carry just hoping to pick myself up. I'll tell myself I can beat the odds. More often than not, I'll fail and teach myself a lesson. Then I'll say, "Well, dummy, you should have laid up." That's the lure of the game. It tempts you to take risks. A consistent golfer gives himself the percentage play most times. He isn't afraid to lay up.

Obviously you have to know how far the carry is to make an intelligent decision. How far is it to carry the hazard and how much farther to your target? Where's the flag?

Here are my rules of thumb for laying up:

- *Lay up to your favorite club.* Most people have a favorite short iron, an 8-iron say. Lay up so you can hit that club for your next shot.
- *Lay up so you can shoot up the slope of the green.* Don't just think about laying up short of trouble, think "angle." On the 15th hole at

Augusta National you will see the pros lay up left and short of the water in front of the green. They lay up left because the green is shallow and slopes sharply from right to left. Give yourself a backstop for your shot into the green.

- *Lay up to a flat lie.* If you have a choice of being 20 yards closer to the green with a sidehill lie or 20 yards back on a level lie, choose the level lie. Do everything you can to make your next shot easier.
- *Lay up to a full shot.* The pros generally prefer to leave themselves a full shot to the green rather than a partial shot, especially if the green is firm. We'd rather hit a full wedge than a half wedge, to put a maximum amount of backspin on the ball and stop it. I think all of us, pros and amateurs alike, find it easier to make a full swing than a half swing. So don't just fire your lay-up shot as far as you can. You probably will be better off 90 yards from the flag than 45 yards.

Once you commit to laying up, make sure you lay up with room to spare. No prizes are awarded for laying up closest to the water. Often you will relax when you make a lay-up swing and hit the ball more squarely. (There is a moral there.)

And always pick a target. Don't say to yourself, "I can't get there, so I'll just take a 7-iron and lay it up." Is the 7-iron the right club for distance? Which side of the fairway do you need to be on for your next shot? If the flag's on the left side of the green and the wind's blowing hard from left to right, lay up to the right—in the right rough perhaps. You'll have the most green to work with. Don't just rifle it up the left side and then wind up lamenting, "Damn, now I have a tough shot, why didn't I think of this before?"

A GREAT CASE OF RISK/REWARD

The 13th at Augusta National is my favorite example of a great risk/reward hole where you may well want to lay up. It's a par 5 that doglegs sharply left, 465 yards from the tournament tees and 435 from the member tees—not long but scary. I've made eagle and I've made double bogey here under pressure. A creek runs up the left side and winds in front of the big green, which slopes hard from left to right. Left of the green is a deep swale.

Ben Crenshaw laid up here all four rounds when he won the Masters. Nick Price laid up when he shot a course-record 63—laid up to his favorite 95-yard distance for a full sand wedge. But Curtis Strange pretty much lost the Masters when he hit it in the water going for the green with a 4-wood.

It's an easy par if you keep the ball out to the right on your first two

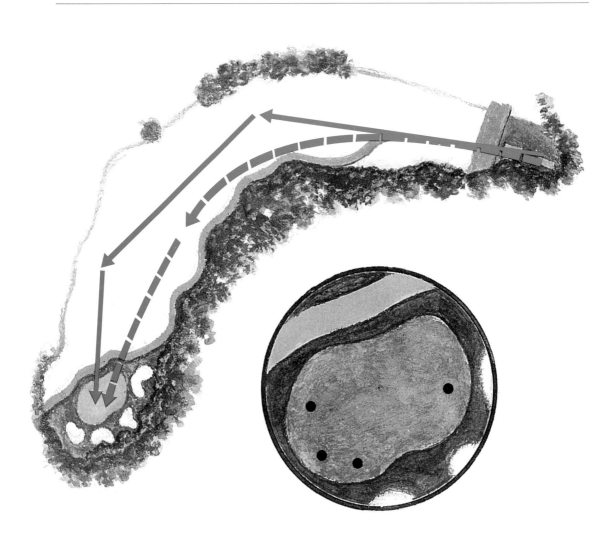

The 13th at Augusta National is a classic gambling hole. Note the typical tournament flag positions.

shots. There's an abundance of room, and the ground slopes from right to left. For the average player who takes the longer but safer route out to the right, it's a driver, a 6-iron or 7-iron lay up and a wedge.

But the beauty of the hole (besides the stunning flora and fauna) is that running a dangerous risk can earn you a generous reward. If you can hook your tee shot around the corner and shorten the hole, you have a shot at eagle. I've gotten home with a middle iron. But if you hook it too much, you're in the creek or the woods and you can make anything. At best you'll have a difficult downhill-sidehill lie for your second shot.

Then you usually have to decide whether to gamble on a long shot to the green, carrying the rocky creek. I played with Crenshaw the first two rounds when he won in 1984. I hit a tee shot through the fairway Saturday at 13 and I had a mediocre lie on pine needles. I was 210 to the front of the green and had to go through two pine trees. It was a shot I logically could have laid up but I was struggling, just staying in the chase, and felt I needed to make something happen. I hit a flush shot with a 4-wood and knocked it right in the middle of the green, a beautiful shot. As the ball was in the air, lightning flashed several times. I'll never forget it. I remember a dog barking in fright. That was the last shot we hit that day because of the storm. But that shot gave me a lift and I wound up finishing second to Ben. It was a risky shot that paid a huge reward.

If you choose to lay up, mentally divide the green in half, left side and right side. If the flag is on the right, lay up to the left. If the flag is on the left, lay up to the right.

The most difficult hole position is on the right front. I don't go for the green in two when the flag's up front since Jack Nicklaus redesigned it (I don't care for the change). You definitely need to leave yourself a full shot to that right-front position, not a 45-yard wedge. You need a lot of spin on the ball to stop it, because the green is quite firm and flat down there—it doesn't cant from back to front in that area. Ideally you want enough backspin to carry the ball close to the flag and stop it quickly. You don't want to carry the ball just onto the green, because it's liable to wind up in the creek.

If the flag is on the tiny shelf that Nicklaus built at the back left, I depart from my usual strategy of leaving myself a full third shot. The farther up the right side of the fairway I can hit my second shot, the better third shot I will have. If I lay back 90 or 100 yards, I have to shoot over the point of Jack's shelf and the ball can kick either right or left when it lands. Left is a deep swale that's a tough challenge.

Laying up close to the creek on the right will give me a simple pitch straight up the face of the slope. I can land the ball on the lower tier and run it up to the hole with no problem. I see a lot of players lay back with their second shots when the flag's on the back left, but that's the wrong place for a pro. However, my way is a riskier lay up. I have to hit the ball past the creek where it fronts the green, then pitch over the creek. You have to judge carefully the bounce of your lay-up shot when it lands, and you will face a downhill lie for your short pitch onto the green.

The hole presents a wonderful range of possibilities. You need to understand them to play it intelligently.

CHAPTER 8
Good Out!

We find ourselves in the rough or the trees occasionally despite our best planning. It's that kind of game. The trick is to control the damage. Don't let one bad stroke lead to another. Get out of trouble in one stroke so you don't bring on a disaster hole.

The main thing in heavy rough is to take a club with enough loft to get the ball up and out quickly. Take more loft than you think you need. If that means hitting a sand wedge sideways, reconcile yourself to giving up yardage to be sure you are out in the fairway for your next shot. The worst tendency is to try a heroic shot—and leave the ball in the rough. I know a top teacher who counsels 18-handicappers never to use more than a 5-iron out of the rough. The long-term odds are much better.

Long irons are almost useless in bad rough. The heavy grass shuts down the clubface and makes it too hard to hit the ball in the air. Don't rule out your shorter irons if you have a sunken lie. Be sure you put the ball back in play, even if you have to give up a stroke.

Your swing needs to be more vertical than usual. You want the club moving in and out of the rough as efficiently as possible, so it doesn't get hung up in the grass. Stand a little closer to the ball to make a more upright swing. A slice swing is actually good. Take the club outside your target line and up with an open face. The grass is going to close the face anyway. You will lose distance, but remember that your objective is to escape the rough. A flat swing makes the club grab too much grass.

The shot probably will come out low and run more than usual, even though you've taken measures to get it up. Allow for that.

I loosen my hands a bit playing long shots out of the rough, for faster hand action at the bottom of my swing. I want a lot of "play" in my hands so I can accelerate the club in and out of the rough.

On tour we play mainly out of bluegrass and Bermuda-grass rough. Bermuda is the worst because it's wiry and stops the club more. If I have a bad lie in Bermuda rough, I'll hit the ball quite a bit harder. I'll still play the shot with an open face and an upright swing.

I always will try to hit a few extra shots out of the rough in a practice round...long shots and also short shots around the green. I want to learn how hard I have to swing to hit the ball different distances.

At the least you should take a couple of serious practice swings before you play a shot out of the rough. Find a patch of grass similar to your lie and swing the club through it. Visualize your club swinging through to a high finish. Just be sure you don't move your ball by mistake and suffer a penalty stroke.

SET CLUB ON TOE FROM GREENSIDE ROUGH

For pitch and chip shots from rough around the green, I set my sand wedge on the toe at address, especially in heavy U.S. Open type rough. I raise my hands to set the club on its toe.

It's easier to get the ball up in the air. There's less bounce in play with

CHAPTER 9
Which Short Shot Hits the Spot?

Alot of strategy goes into shots around the green too. I practice and preach hitting to a spot on short shots. It's my No. 1 tactic. I placed different clubs on the ground posing for this artwork on the facing page to demonstrate various options.

The ball closer to the hole is several feet off the green on the short fringe or froghair. I laid down a putter, a 5-iron and a sand wedge. What's your choice?

I've seen the shot played with all these clubs on tour. Raymond Floyd chips it from this distance all the time and very effectively. But I always would putt the ball, and I suggest you do the same. The 5-iron would be my second choice, the sand wedge my last. Invariably my worst putt is better than my worst chip on a smooth surface. I have more control with the putter. My stroke is simpler, and the ball behaves more predictably.

But I'm giving you a choice. If you chip the ball, chip it to land on a spot and roll to the hole like a putt. I visualize a chip shot as a chip and putt combined. If you chip with the 5-iron, land the ball on the near spot. If you take the sand wedge, land it on the far spot.

The other ball is 10 feet farther off the green. I put down a 7-iron and a 60-degree wedge. If you use the 7-iron, land the ball on the first spot and let it run to the hole. If you use the wedge, land it on the second spot. I'd prefer the 7-iron because there's more margin for error.

When I was young, I played all my shots near the green with a wedge. I was good at popping the ball up. But the older I get, the less I can count on that great touch and the more I want the ball rolling on the green. Generally it's better to turn these shots into putts as soon as possible.

Whatever you do, hit to a spot. Visualize landing the ball on that spot. Then it's just a question of judging how the ball will travel as a putt. If you commit to playing to a spot, and practice it, your scoring should improve dramatically.

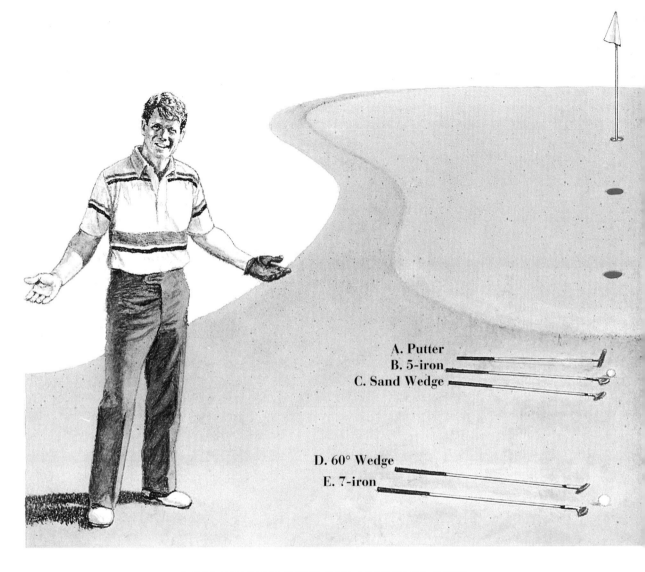

A. Putter
B. 5-iron
C. Sand Wedge

D. 60° Wedge
E. 7-iron

USE LESS LOFT ON AN UPSLOPE

The short shot I see misplayed the most is the one off a severe upslope. It's too hard to hit to a spot because players, even good ones, select a club with too much loft, often a wedge. The ball lands short and comes up well short of the hole. What people fail to appreciate is that 15 to 20 degrees of loft already is built into the slope! Add that to the loft on a wedge and the ball jumps almost straight up in the air!

Use the upslope. Select a less lofted club, a 7-iron or 6-iron. Judging the distance will be much easier. It's simpler to hit to a spot off an upslope

Select a less lofted club off an upslope.

with a less lofted club, because the trajectory is flatter and you're making a shorter swing. Uphill, align your shoulders and body with the slope and position the ball forward in your stance. Downhill, reverse all of the above and allow for more roll on the green. In either case, play to a spot, from where the ball can roll like a putt.

FROM ROUGH, PLAY TO THE SAFER SPOT

You'll recognize this little tester. You're in the rough 35 feet off the green and you have a moderate amount of green to work with. Your choices are an 8-iron to a spot just on the green or a sand wedge to a second spot 15 feet onto the green. For once, the less lofted club is more dangerous. If you hit the ball a little heavy, you easily could land short in the high grass and fail to get on the green.

A good wedge player is at a big advantage here. He'll always carry the ball well onto the green and get it close.

KEY ON THE SPOT, NOT THE TROUBLE

We've been talking about options. Here's a shot that gives you no option. You're about 60 feet from the hole. You have to lob the ball out of the rough, over a bunker, downhill to a tight pin position.

I choose a sand wedge. Now I mentally block out the bunker and focus on the spot where I want to land the ball. In this instance it's in the fringe. Otherwise I have no chance to stop the ball on the green. My main swing thought is to keep the knuckles of my left hand pointing to the sky through the ball. That holds the clubface open and gets the ball up quickly and down softly.

Good luck!

CHAPTER 10
How to Play the Bump-and-Run

Ilove the British Open for the bump-and-run shots you play. St. Andrews, golf's grand old lady, is extra special. Chipping and running the ball is a style of play I didn't like at first, because I thought too much luck was involved, but I've come to consider it the ultimate.

On our tour we play soft courses that force you to fly the ball onto the

Here's a bump-and-run situation you encounter often. Land the ball on a flat spot so you can gauge its bounce and roll more accurately.

green. In Britain they play firmer courses that call for more inventive shot-making into and around the green, which often is open in front. The ground is hard and you want to bounce and roll the ball onto the green in many cases.

Bump-and-run golf is often the way you should play when the weather is poor. For example, downwind with the pin cut close to the front of an open green behind a mound, you probably can't get the ball close unless you run it.

Isao Aoki is a master of the tactic, and is especially adept at playing the difficult chip-and-run going uphill through grainy grass. I always think he's hit the ball way too hard, but he has the shot figured. The grain checks the ball some, but the ball bounces through. Going downhill, the grain normally slopes away from you. Isao is wonderful at getting the ball to just trickle over the top of a mound and roll smoothly down the other side.

Americans rely far too little on the bump-and-run. On dry courses

without a lot of rough, the average weekend player would improve his up-and-down percentage by trying more ground shots and fewer finesse wedges. I will play a bump-and-run shot any time I have the opening and don't think I have enough room to land the ball on the green and stop it within 25 feet of the hole.

EXAMPLES FROM ST. ANDREWS

The sixth hole has a dip in front of the green. You have to judge where to chip the ball so it lands short of the green, bounces up the bank and then rolls down the other side.

On the 12th hole, a short par 4, there's a little plateau in the middle of the green where they always put the pin. Downwind you have to play your second shot short of the green and run it up onto that plateau.

The 18th is famous for the Valley of Sin at the front left of the green. Doug Sanders lost the Open trying to hit a high wedge in there. He ended up well beyond the hole and three-putted. Because Doug was a master of the bump-and-run shot, there is still a lot of conjecture among the players whether he should have run the ball through the Valley of Sin.

AVOID LANDING ON SLOPES

Slope is a major factor playing the bump-and-run. I always prefer to land the ball on a flat area for greater control. I avoid sideslopes like wild animals, because you never can be sure how the ball will kick.

Upslopes and downslopes you can handle more easily. Take a less lofted club into an upslope, a more lofted club into a downslope. Wind is another factor. You may well need less club than you think going downwind and more club upwind.

The big key to the bump-and-run: Pick the spot where you want to land the ball and then pick the club that will carry it to that spot and bounce and run it to your target.

Don't try a bump-and-run shot through lush, long grass. But under dry, firm conditions, the bump-and-run often is your smartest choice.

This is the most common bump-and-run situation. I'm short of the green and the pin is near the front edge. I want to bounce and roll the ball over a mound and be able to stop it near the hole. Using a basic chipping stroke, I land the ball in a flat "valley" so the ball will have the forward momentum to get up the slope. Usually I try to bounce the ball twice before it gets to the green. The first bounce takes the steam off the shot, the second bounce gets the ball rolling. I want the ball rolling smoothly down the slope like a putt.

You have to hit the ball harder than you think to get it up the slope.

WHEN YOU MISS ON THE SHORT SIDE

We all know this little nightmare of a shot. The green is elevated and you've missed it on the wrong side. You have only a few feet of green to the pin. Unless you can hit the ball straight up in the air with a sand wedge, you almost have to play a bump-and-run. My dad is a poor wedge player who has played this shot for years with a middle iron and consistently leaves himself a reasonable putt. If the grass is heavy, hit the ball higher into the slope with a more lofted club and play for a big first bounce. If the grass is short, hit the ball lower into the slope with a less lofted club. Likewise, you hit the ball higher into a softer slope, lower into a firmer slope. Either way, you may have to hit the ball harder than you think to get it up and onto the green.

CHAPTER 11
Overestimate the Wind

Wind is the most unpredictable factor in golf. It also is the most underestimated. And you have to consider wind on most of your shots. It's often a major influence on scoring.

Most golfers underplay the wind—dramatically. They adjust by a club or two clubs into the wind or downwind, when they should adjust by three or four clubs or even more. A 20-mile-an-hour headwind will shorten my normal drive of 270 yards by 40 yards! A 20-mile-an-hour tailwind will lengthen it by 20 yards. And wait till I tell you later in this chapter what a crosswind does to your slice.

These diagrams show what happens to my tee shot with a driver when the wind is hurting or helping. A high 3-wood can be a better choice downwind.

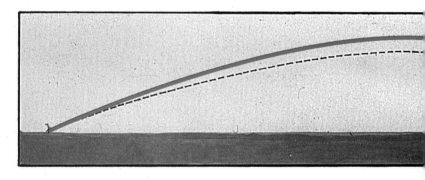

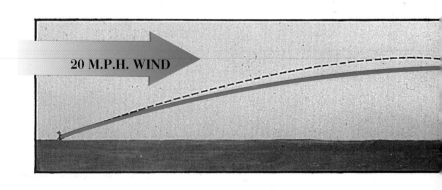

20 M.P.H. WIND

20 M.P.H. WIND

230 yards   270 yards

270 yards   290 yards

Frank Thomas and the technical people at the U.S. Golf Association recently quantified for me my belief that the effect of the wind is much greater than most people think. They quote the results of computerized simulations, using a three-dimensional trajectory model they developed from actual test data. The numbers that result are for a representative ball.

Downhill the effect of the wind will be greater because the ball's in the air longer. Uphill, the effect of the wind will be less.

A headwind holds the ball up longer, and a tailwind knocks it down. A 5-iron has a hang time of 7.6 seconds upwind, 6.1 downwind. When the wind is behind you, the extra roll can be considerable, even with a short iron. One day at Gleneagles in Scotland on firm turf, I drove the ball downwind 494 yards by actual measurement. Greg Norman still kids me that he hit it 486 that day and was outdriven.

Norman is a good wind player. Lee Trevino is excellent. So are Ray Floyd and Arnold Palmer. They rarely underestimate the influence of the wind.

Once you diagnose the wind and pick the correct club, the key is to put the ball cleanly on the clubface. You always want to meet the ball squarely, but it's especially important in the wind, where the effect on a mis-hit is drastic. Good swing tempo is essential.

Don't let the wind rush you into a quick swing, which is the tendency. When swinging in the wind, I swing easier at the ball. One of Golf Digest's old one-page tips was titled "Swing with ease against a breeze." That's a good one to remember.

Downwind I might take less club for an approach shot and hit the ball harder if I'm playing well, because it will spin more and stop better on the green. But that's the only time I'll swing harder.

I try to hit the ball higher going downwind. A high 3-wood can work better off the tee than a driver, because you get better carry.

I will tee the ball a little higher going downwind. I don't mind hitting the ball toward the top of the clubface with the driver. You have to get the ball up in the air so it can blow with the wind. Into the wind, I'll tee the ball a little lower.

Being a high-ball hitter, I like to hit the ball lower into the wind. I move the ball back in my stance and play it about an inch closer to my body, being sure the clubface is aimed square to the target. Then I try to finish low with my swing.

When the wind is really blowing hard, one of the things you ought to do is shorten your swing. And one of the easiest ways to shorten your swing is to widen your stance. It is harder to make a big swing with a wider stance. I angle both feet out in a big wind. My turn will be

Widen your stance in a strong wind.

restricted, and my balance will be better. Watch good wind players like Floyd and Trevino. They widen their stances in the wind.

Gusting wind is the worst. That's why 64 balls went in the water on the 17th hole one day at The Players Championship a few years ago. In conditions like that, all you can do is hit the ball solidly and hope the wind doesn't change as you play the shot.

The trickiest wind in golf for me is on the 12th hole at the Masters Tournament, the diabolical little 155-yard par 3. You're never sure where the wind is coming from, and it swirls unpredictably. It can shift on you in mid-swing. It might feel downwind at the tee and be upwind at the green. You have to make excellent judgments there.

When the wind blows a gale I'm glad I'm 5-9 instead of 6-4. But sometimes I wish I weighed 50 pounds more.

COPING WITH A CROSSWIND

Keeping the ball in play in a heavy crosswind demands special strategy. My advice to better players is to work the ball into the wind to get a straight shot. Slice the ball into a right-to-left wind or hook the ball into a left-to-right wind.

This assumes a certain shotmaking ability. If you cannot hook and slice the ball on call, take your chances letting the wind maneuver the ball for you. In a left-to-right crosswind, aim down the left side of the hole. The trouble with this approach is that your target area is drastically reduced, because the ball is going to land moving at an angle from left to right and then bounce and run that way. If the ground is hard, the ball easily can scurry into the rough, or worse. If you are inclined to slice the ball anyway, beware! Aim well left—left of the fairway perhaps.

On average, a 25-yard slice will slice another 25 yards with a left-to-right wind blowing 20 miles per hour! Your error is doubled to 50 yards!

Downhill the wind's effect on curvature will be greater when you use the wind. The longer the ball's in the air, the more it's going to curve. Going uphill you can play a somewhat straighter shot.

I will hook the ball into a left-to-right wind—hook it a lot if the wind's blowing hard. If I calculate properly, the amount the ball is hooking will offset the speed of the crosswind. Working the ball into a crosswind is a fairly advanced way to play, but the most effective in my view.

I think of banking my shot into a wall of wind. That wall is going to knock the ball down, so I'm going to lose some distance. Hooking a drive into a 20-mile-an-hour crosswind will shorten my carry by 10 yards, but my shot will be straighter.

Be aware of the pin position hitting to the green. And beware if the pin's on the windward side of the green. Don't miss the green on that side or else you will face a sticky downwind recovery shot. In other words, if the wind is from right to left and the pin is on the right, don't miss the green to the right.

JUDGING WIND DIRECTION

If there's water nearby, I use that to figure the wind. The windward side of the lake will be calm. The leeward side will be choppy. I'll also look at the treetops, toss grass in the air and observe other players' shots—but I like to check water. If I'm looking from the tee to the green on the 17th hole of the Tournament Players Club in Florida with the wind in my face, the water will be rough near the tee and smooth near the green. If the wind's behind me, the water will be smooth near the tee. The bank shields the upwind side of the lake.

CHAPTER 12
The 30-Minute Warm-Up

Weekend golfers often start a round badly and may not recover because they don't warm up well or don't know how to get their swings from the practice tee to the first tee. Do you allow enough time to prepare yourself to play? I don't see how you can get ready in less than 30 minutes, minimum.

You would never see a baseball, football or basketball player fail to warm up thoroughly before a game, and yet weekend golfers seldom spend enough time warming up. I know you probably are pressed for time, but if you are going to spend most of a day at the golf course it's well worth it to get there 30 minutes early. It can be the difference between a good round and a poor one, between making money on the bets and losing money.

If half an hour was all I had, I'd spend five minutes putting, including some long putts to gauge the speed of the greens, then 10 minutes chipping and pitching. Your short-game feel is most important. Finally I'd spend 15 minutes hitting balls on the range.

Actually my preparation for a round begins when I get out of bed in the morning. I try to do everything deliberately before I get to the course. I brush my teeth slowly, eat slowly, drive the car slowly. If you feel you're doing everything slowly when you're pumped up on game day, you probably will be going at about normal pace. I've heard that Bobby Locke, the fine South African player, would take several minutes to tie his shoelaces in the morning. He wanted to establish an unhurried tempo right away.

Within 20 minutes of your tee time, you should do a few minutes of golf-related stretches, to get your body ready and to avoid injury. The older I get, the more stretches I do. I now do 10 different ones for a total of at least 10 minutes. Several are based on an excellent little manual called "30 Exercises for Better Golf" by the Centinela Hospital Medical Center which works with our tour.

Here's one I use faithfully. It stretches the back part of your shoulder. (The left side is active swinging back and the right side is active swinging down and through.) Stretch your arm across your chest as far as you comfortably can without turning your body, and hold that position for 10 seconds, bracing your arm and helping it into a fully stretched position with your opposite hand.

Stretch your shoulders, stretch your neck, stretch your hamstrings, stretch your back. Stretch everything that comes into play in your golf swing. Stretch a muscle slowly and gently. You'll find your overall flexibility increasing as you do more stretching. And if you're a slow starter on the course, you'll likely find yourself getting off to a faster start after stretching.

Once I'm on the practice tee, I take my time going from one ball to the next. I keep one simple swing key in mind: It might be swing in balance, or keep my head quiet. It's a form of self-discipline and I'm getting in quality practice time as I warm up.

Occasionally I see some of you hit too many balls warming up. You hit

I prefer to warm up and practice with the sun behind me.
I can check my shadow for excessive body movement during the swing.

a hundred balls and then burn out in the middle of the round. Hitting too many balls also can wear the feel out of your hands and hurt your putting.

Whenever possible I like to warm up and practice with the sun behind me so my shadow is out in front of me. My peripheral vision tells me if I'm swaying off the ball with my upper body on the backswing. I want to turn my right hip out of the way early in my swing, and hitting balls with the sun behind me lets me check myself. The shadow also helps me stay behind the ball with my upper body through impact. Your sense of hearing is another aid. It can tell you how solidly you're making contact with the ball. I have a blind friend in Japan who can listen to me hit balls and report which ones are cleanly struck. The good ones coming off an iron have that nice hissing sound. The ball almost sticks to the clubface.

I hit each ball to a target, to simulate real conditions. I concentrate on where I want the ball to land. To get a sense for judging distance as you warm up, hit different clubs to a practice flag. If the flag is 150 yards and you'd normally hit a 6-iron, try a 7-iron and a 5-iron, too. Conditions vary every day.

They also vary with you and your swing. You never feel or swing quite the same from one day to the next.

Hit one club for a while and work on shaping your shots. Hit some fades and some draws.

See how your shot-shaping tendencies might affect your round. Some days it's easier to move the ball one way versus the other. You have to go with that tendency rather than fight it. If you pull your fade attempts, you might want to aim more left when you need to hit a fade during your round.

During my warm-up I'll work on a few key shots I know I'll face on this particular course. Every course has them, and you don't want to try a shot in competition you haven't tried in practice.

An example would be the long, par-3 16th hole over the ocean at Cypress Point. Many times it is a 3-wood or even a driver. You have to know where the wind is coming from on that hole. If it's blowing from left to right, I will practice a draw in my warm-up, so the ball goes out there and stays straight. If the wind's blowing from right to left, I'll work on an intentional fade.

If I feel I'll have to play some critical three-quarter shots with a sand wedge on the course, I'll be sure to hit some while warming up, with an open blade, with a closed blade. I want to anticipate the key shots I'll get during the round and be ready for them.

Notice where the wind is and figure what bearing it might have on your first tee shot. If there's a large American flag flying at the clubhouse, it probably can tell you what the wind's doing. It's especially useful to know the wind on a mountain course where it might be blocked at the tee but will influence the ball greatly once the ball gets past a slope.

FINISH YOUR WARM-UP WITH A DRIVER

I see more and more tour pros changing their pre-round warm-up routine to go directly from hitting the driver on the practice tee to hitting the driver on the first tee. It's simple logic.

Most weekend golfers will go to the range, then to the putting green, then to the first tee. They warm up on the range, cool down on the putting green and have to warm up again to tee off.

It makes sense to practice your short game first, then go to the practice tee and work up from your short irons to the driver, the club you will use to start your round. The last warm-up shot you play should be with your driver. Play it the way you want to play it off the first tee—slice it, hook it, whatever. Then you are physically and mentally prepared for that crucial opening drive.

Always finish your warm-up with a good hit, not a mis-hit. That sends you to the first tee with confidence.

The pros tend to cut it tight getting to the tee on time, going as straight as they can from hitting a driver on the range to hitting a driver on the first tee. It's a good way to get your swing from the practice tee to the first tee.

THAT SCARY FIRST DRIVE

I believe it's the most critical shot of the round. It sets the mental tone. If you drive the ball well, you know you can play well that day. Instant momentum. If you don't drive it well, you may need several holes to generate confidence.

Understand that all of us are nervous on the first tee. The new players at the Masters every year always talk about how they're not sure they can tee up the ball, their hands are shaking so badly. I remember walking up the first fairway at Augusta National years ago with Johnny Miller, and he said he was so nervous he didn't even feel the hill. That is a very steep hill.

If I'm designing a course, I like the first tee shot to be relatively wide open, so everybody at least has a good chance to get the round started on a positive note. I prefer a short or medium-length par 4 that isn't too tight or troubled.

What can you do to relax on the first tee, in front of a bunch of onlookers, with your motor barely running?

Use deep-breathing exercises to calm your nerves. Realize that every-

A good way to get your swing from the practice tee to the first tee is to rehearse your opening drive on the range.

body else is nervous, the same as you. I'm more nervous on the opening tee shot than almost any other shot, including a pressure shot down the stretch. It's normal and shows you're alert and ready to compete.

Concentrate as hard as you can on putting the ball in play. Aim away from hazards. If you haven't warmed up enough, just swing with rhythm. Wait until later in the round to hit the ball hard. Swing the clubhead with good rhythm. Feel the clubhead.

I want to hit the ball squarely on the clubface and get it in play.

CHAPTER 13

How to Play a Practice Round

Scheduling a practice round before you play in an event can make a telling difference in how you fare. A tour pro gets in at least one practice round prior to a tournament, even on a course he's played before.

You use a practice round to formulate your game plan. Let's take as an example Augusta National, where the Masters Tournament is played each year. Because most of the holes there dogleg from right to left, I'll practice hitting a draw with my driver getting ready for the Masters.

I'll take you with me on a tour of Augusta's famous back nine in a few moments.

During a practice round, generally speaking, I want to find out where the trouble is and where the bail-out areas are. On a strange course I won't walk directly to my ball; I'll walk alongside the trouble areas like a surveyor, to see how far they extend and which way the ground slants.

I want to learn where I can and cannot miss a shot. If I do miss a shot, I want to be sure I can recover and not incur a big score on the hole.

I need to find out when I will want to lay up and when I won't. When should I gamble and when shouldn't I? The answer will be influenced by what's happening in the tournament, but also by my advance study of the course.

I'll walk briskly around the greens on a practice round. I'm checking for the best areas to pitch or chip from if I should miss the green, and I'm observing the general slopes that are going to affect putts the most.

I'll hit more recovery shots than putts in practice rounds. Nobody hits every green, and you have to know the best places to recover from. You pretty much know where the pins will be during the tournament and you play to those areas in your practice rounds.

Here are other things I look for on a practice round.

THE GREENS

It's most important to determine the consistency and speed of the greens, because both your putting and club selection are impacted. If the greens

are soft and slow, you can play your approach shots more aggressively—maybe shoot right at the flagstick. If the greens are firm and fast, you have to aim more cautiously and concentrate on your distance control.

Determine whether the greens are similar in pace from one to the next. And whether the practice green putts like the regular greens. Sometimes the practice green can fool you. Lee Trevino says he often finds the practice green faster than the greens on the course.

THE FAIRWAYS

How consistent are they? How short are they cut? Do I have to guard against hitting flyers, where the ball takes off on me from a grassy lie?

THE ROUGH

What will I be able to do out of the rough? At the Tournament of Champions, the rough looks very deep, but there's a cushion of grass under the long grass and the ball will sit on top of that cushion. You can take more chances.

But when the PGA Championship was at Shoal Creek, the rough was only three inches deep and the ball sank to the bottom. Often you could only wedge it out.

THE WIND

What is the prevailing wind?

I might carry a 4-wood in my bag if I need to carry the ball a long way and high, but a 1-iron if I have to keep the ball lower and straighter.

How will the wind affect the play of different holes? The wind at Augusta often determines whether you go for the green in two on the par-5 holes.

Is the wind apt to change in mid-round? Listen to the weather reports and adjust in a way that makes sense for you.

THE SAND

I want to ascertain whether the sand is fine or coarse. Soft or firm, is it wet—has it been raining? Will the ball plug? If it will plug in a soft area of sand in front of a particular pin position, you might want to shoot away from that pin.

At the Masters I try to play two or three warm-up rounds. The greens are terribly challenging, and you have to know them as well as you know your best friends to win. The problem in getting used to them is that they usually get faster as the week goes along.

I seldom play for a score in practice rounds. Sometimes I will miss a green intentionally to see what kind of recovery shot I leave myself from a certain position. You are allowed to play only one ball at Augusta, to protect the turf, but if you miss a green you generally hit another approach shot and no one complains.

Here's how my mind works on the back nine at Augusta during a practice round. Hopefully this rundown will give you a better appreciation of these holes watching the Masters on television.

No. 10. It's a 485-yard par 4, but it plays sharply downhill. The hole calls for a right-to-left draw off the tee. If you can hit a low draw that catches the downslope on the left side of the fairway, the ball will run a lot farther. But you're flirting with the tree line.

You don't want to miss your second shot to the right. You can miss left and recover much more easily. I will work on pitch and chip shots from left of the green.

The green is very sloping and is maybe the firmest and toughest to putt on the course, because it's in the shade and the grass is thin. You just try to get a long putt within four feet of the hole.

No. 11. The second shot is the key. The right side is the safe side, away from the water. In practice I chip from right of the green, reminding myself that the green runs away from me toward the water. I take extra putts from the front right of the green to the left pin positions.

No. 12. This is the shortest hole on the course and the most dangerous. It's even harder than the 16th at Cypress Point. The wind is the toughest I've ever had to figure.

You want to miss over the green rather than short and in the water, so you practice out of the gully and out of the bunkers in back. Fred Couples was extremely fortunate his ball stopped on the bank and didn't roll back into the water the last round in 1992. The bank wasn't mowed because the course got so much rain before the round.

No. 13. I don't go for the green as readily as I did before it was flattened out in front. If the pin's in the front, you can't stop the ball close to the hole when hitting a long shot from a sidehill lie in the fairway.

I practice from the deep depression left of the green and also I putt up to the left plateau and down from it.

No. 14. The fact it has no bunker doesn't make it simple. The green is severely mounded.

Your approach shot has to clear the front mound or the ball will come back off the green and you'll face a terribly hard chip. The best misses are long and right. I will chip from there on my practice rounds.

No. 15. It's the last realistic chance for an eagle, so you often go for it down the stretch. You need a long drive and a solid second shot to reach the green in two. Depending on the wind, the approach can be anything from a middle iron to a fairway wood.

If I lay up, I want to be to the left, where the angle up the green is better. I avoid the left side of the green—it's a hogback, and the ball can run through into the water on 16.

The putt from the right side of the green to the left is deceptively fast, and I make sure to test its speed.

No. 16. The right part of the green is raised, and I play a lot of practice putts from the left side up to the right back. Also a couple of shots from the right bunker.

No. 17. I have to practice from a buried lie in the front bunker, because I'm always in there. I will chip from over the green to the front right of the green.

No. 18. It's a tight hole, but usually I prefer to hit a driver and give myself the shortest club possible into a green that slopes treacherously from back to front. The danger with the driver is that you can knock the ball into the deep bunkers to the left if you don't fade it. But especially if the pin is on the back of the green I want to hit a short iron and have a chance of stopping the ball up there. (When the greens are holding, a middle iron can land on top and roll all the way back off the front of the green.)

If I'm leading the tournament the final day, however, I probably will lay up off the tee with a fairway wood, to be sure of avoiding the fairway bunkers. Then if I'm hitting a middle iron to a back pin position, I will land the ball on the front of the green and let it bounce and roll up the slope. The longer the club, the lower you can hit it.

I'll try these different combinations in my practice rounds.

The broad game plan that has served me best at Augusta over the years is simply to tell myself that *I must not hit two bad shots in a row.* I know I will hit some bad shots on that great course under Masters pressure, as will everyone else. But I vow never to follow a bad shot with another bad shot.

CHAPTER 14
Match Play and Other Formats

Your strategy depends greatly on what game you're playing. Are you playing stroke play or match play? Are you playing as an individual or as part of a team? Are you playing a foursome or four-ball? Stableford or skins? Each of those formats changes your tactics.

Most of the time I play stroke play, where every shot is counted. It's the most rigorous test, and that's why we play it for money. You rely only on yourself; you can't blame anything on a partner. Consequently you play more carefully.

But most players choose match play when they compete against each other, probably for nassau bets. You take more chances in match play, and your risk/reward decisions depend partly on what your opponent is doing. That's why I enjoy match play more. That's why the Ryder Cup is so exciting.

In match play, the play of my opponent often tells me when to be aggressive and when not to be. If he's in trouble, I play safely. If I'm in trouble, I can play more aggressively.

Let's use the famous 18th hole at Pebble Beach as an example. It's a 548-yard par 5, seldom reachable in two, with the ocean running all the way up the left side. If my opponent hooks his drive into the water and has to re-tee, I'm going to tee off with a 3-iron instead of a driver, aiming away from the water at the two trees in the right center of the fairway. Billy Casper teed off with a 3-iron one year in winning the Crosby. You want all the percentages in your corner when your opponent's in trouble.

If you were playing from the forward tees, you might want to hit even less club to be sure you put the ball in play. This hole, like many par-5 holes, can be negotiated with three iron shots. If my opponent is in trouble, that's how I'd play it. You take more chances in match play, but you also have to know when to play conservatively.

Sometimes you simply have to go for it. If your opponent hits his approach shot close to the hole, you probably have to go for the flag. But every shot has its own risk/reward factor. If it's a par 5 and your opponent hits a great shot to reach the green in two, do you then go for it—or do you lay up and try to wedge it in there close and force him to make his putt to win the hole? Ask yourself how you are hitting the ball. How confident are you in your fairway wood? In your wedge?

I'd rather hit second in match play, no matter what my opponent does. I want all the information possible at my disposal. I know what I have to do. If he hits a terrific shot, I know I have to hit a terrific shot. If he gets in trouble, my options change—I'll play safely most of the time. I won't aim the ball anywhere near a hazard. I've always wanted to hit last in a playoff so I know what everybody else is doing. I have more options.

I hear players say they want to hit first to put the pressure on. Not me. I remember playing a down-home match against Byron Nelson. I hit an approach shot a foot from the hole and said to him, "I got you now." He just said, "There's room inside that." He liked knowing what he had to do. He had to take a risk, but the decision was simple. He'd eliminated a variable because his opponent had dictated what he had to do.

Always watch your opponent play his shot. It can help your play. Notice what iron he pulls out of the bag and how he hits it. See what the wind does to his shot. See how the ball bounces and rolls. It's mightily important around the green and putting. When you prepare for your own shot, you want to be as fully informed as possible.

Occasionally a highly skilled player might try to play a shot that throws you off, but that's seldom a problem. Dutch Harrison could hit a 3-iron the distance of a 5-iron to fool you into hitting over a green, but you don't have to beat many Dutch Harrisons. Neither do I, fortunately. If you know your own game and pay attention to how your opponent plays his shot, you'll be all right.

It's important in match play to observe your opponent's mannerisms, too. If he or she begins playing faster, that could mean he or she is experiencing greater pressure. You may be able to use the observation to advantage by asking your opponent to putt out a "gimme" putt.

One of the best "matches" I ever played was against Jack Nicklaus the final day of the 1977 British Open at Turnberry in Scotland. It wasn't technically match play, but in effect it was because we were playing head-to-head for the championship. I had a one-stroke lead going to the last hole, a 431-yard par 4. I drove into the fairway with a 1-iron, but Jack pushed his drive way off to the right in the gorse. I had to play my approach shot first, so I walked all the way over to Jack's ball to find out whether it was unplayable. He was six inches from being unplayable, but he had a shot.

Had he been unplayable, it would have affected my strategy. I would have played more conservatively with a one-shot lead. I would have played short of the flag because a bogey would win for me. But knowing he could

If my match play opponent hooks his ball into the water on the 18th hole at Pebble Beach, I will tee off with an iron and aim well right of the water.

play the shot—it was a difficult shot, but he had a full swing at it—and knowing he's a great player from the rough, I had to go ahead and play aggressively. I didn't feel I had the option to play conservatively. I played a 7-iron shot that fortunately stopped three feet from the hole. Sure enough, he ripped the ball out of the rough and onto the right corner of the green with a 9-iron, then made a superb 40-foot putt. I nervously holed my three-footer and won by one.

Always assume your opponent is going to hit a super shot. It often happens in match play when you least expect it, near the end of a match. Don't be surprised and rattled when it does. Walking up to that last green at Turnberry, I told my caddie, Alfie Fyles, that I expected Jack to make his putt. When he sank it I wasn't surprised, and that made my concentration on my three-footer easier.

FOUR-BALL TACTICS

Most of us play four-ball matches. You and I play our two balls against the two balls of Chuck and Nick. The better score of each team, with handicap, wins the hole. A lot of thought can go into who should do what for your side.

One of the charges of a Ryder Cup captain is to pair players who are compatible. People's strengths and weaknesses on a particular golf course have to be considered, with the wind conditions a major factor. It's easy to overanalyze doing pairings. I think the most important thing is how comfortable one player is with another. That can offset a lot of technical-sounding criteria. If I personally have a choice of partners, I always will pick the best putter I can.

Why is the wind such a factor? It can determine who plays and who sits out in the team matches. If the wind is into the players on a long hole with water in front of the green, you might be at a disadvantage pairing two shorter hitters. They might not be able to clear the hazard easily enough. A British Ryder Cup captain once sat out a player for all of the team matches because he didn't feel the player could carry the dune on the 11th hole at Muirfield into the wind.

It isn't a bad idea at any level of the game to pair a big hitter with a shorter, steadier player. Generally I prefer to have the steadier player tee off first. Once he's in the fairway, the big hitter has less pressure to put the ball in play.

The pressure in a match is always fluctuating, though. You have to feel your way through a match. People are nervous teeing off. It can be smart for the straighter hitter to tee off first on the early holes, then switch and let the big hitter lead off on long par 4s and reachable par 5s. If your team is faltering, sometimes it simply helps just to change the order of teeing off for no particular reason.

When you get to the green all sorts of permutations are possible. I like to make opponents putt out everything for the first few holes and at the end of the match. In between, concede a few putts. But feel out your opposition. If they barely lip in or miss short putts early in the round, make them keep putting them all day. Keep the pressure on. But if they're sinking everything dead center, give them those putts for a while, then make them putt them toward the end of the match. My dad taught me this lesson during our championship match in the Walloon Lake Club Championship. We were vacationing in Michigan when I was 14 years old. He gave me all the short putts until the 20th hole, when he made me putt it. You can guess the rest of the story.

A two-foot putt on the last hole will look a lot longer. And you always control whether your opponents do or don't putt out.

Here's a common situation on the green. Your opponents are about 12 feet away for birdies. You are 40 feet for birdie. Your partner is four feet for birdie. Since you are "away" your team has the option to have your partner, who is four feet from the hole, putt first. I usually prefer that my partner putt the four-footer before I try my 40-footer. If he sinks it, he puts extra pressure on the 12-footers.

You see that a lot in Ryder Cup. It happened on the second hole at the Belfry in 1989 when Mark O'Meara and I were playing Seve Ballesteros and Jose Maria Olazabal, the great Spanish team. O'Meara and I both hit our approaches 11 or 12 feet from the hole. Seve had about 40 feet, and Ollie had it four to five feet. Ollie putted first and made it. He's terrific from that distance. We both missed. We went on to get shellacked.

Now, if the man putting the four-footer is putting for par and is a poor short putter—and your opponents have difficult birdie putts from 12 feet—you might want to try the long putt first to secure an odds-on halve. But if your opponents' putts are easy, you are odds-on to lose. Have your partner putt the four-footer first to give you a free run if he makes it.

Another situation, less common. Your two opponents are on the same putting line, and one of their putts doesn't mean anything. Concede them the meaningless putt so they don't learn anything from it. Tell them to pick it up. You can concede a putt in match play to keep your opponents from getting the line. By knowing the rules for match play and how they differ from the rules for stroke play, you can create an advantage. It's acceptable gamesmanship—and it's smart strategy.

USE YOUR STROKES—AND PRESS—SHREWDLY

First, know where your strokes fall on the scorecard. Mark your card before you tee off. You must know where you—and the other side—receive strokes. The ninth and 18th holes usually are get-even holes in a nassau bet. If you get a stroke and the opposition doesn't, you have an advantage and most likely would want to press a bet or add a bet. A press is an extra bet made by the side that's trailing, and only applies to the remaining holes.

On a key hole, assess your strengths and weaknesses and the other side's strengths and weaknesses relative to that hole. If it's a dogleg right and you're a slicer and your opponent's a hooker, you probably have an edge. Or if the cup is cut on a difficult slope and you are the better putter, you have an edge.

Maybe the No. 1 handicap hole isn't all that hard for you and you usually play it well. Maybe it's into the wind and you're a low-ball hitter. You might want to press in the betting. On the other hand, if the hole's into the wind and you typically hit the ball high and make bogey, you probably won't want to press. Play for bogey. Don't gamble on making par. Most opponents are going to have trouble on the No. 1 hole anyway. If you get a stroke and make a net par, the percentages are with you.

If you know your opponent, use that knowledge. Maybe you're giving up a stroke on a hole, but your opponent has a pattern of trying to be too macho on that hole and will have trouble trying to clear a hazard. You may want to press there even though you're giving a stroke. That's good management. Your ego may urge you to try a shot your common sense tells you not to try. Listen to your common sense.

Ordinarily, don't press when you are giving a stroke on a par 3. Press on a par 3 only when you feel you have a clear advantage due to its length, the shape of the shot required or the wind—in relation to your opponent's weaknesses.

If you are a long hitter and are 2 down against a short hitter coming to a reachable par 5, it's a good time to press. If you are coming to a short par 4 against a short, straight hitter, you might want to press later.

Lee Trevino always says, "Never give a guy strokes on his home course." Playing against local knowledge can kill you, even with the new handicapping index system. The home-course player knows which club to pull out of the bag and how the putts break. If you're playing on a course you've never seen before, you'd better negotiate the bets harder.

I like to play a fun game where you can press when the opponent's ball is in the air. If his ball's headed for water or out-of-bounds, you can yell "press!" Any time. If he refuses, he pays the original bet. If he accepts, the bet is doubled. It's similar to the doubling cube in backgammon.

In the more common formats, remember that you don't have to accept a press unless it's been defined as automatic. It isn't uncommon to decline—and furthermore it can frustrate the other side.

ALTERNATE-SHOT TACTICS

Foursomes (or alternate shot) is another stimulating format. We should play more of it in this country. It's a fast and fun game. In Ryder Cup, if I'm on the tee, my partner can go on out near the driving zone and be ready to play the next shot. The British play foursomes almost entirely at their clubs on busy weekends. They'll go around in the morning in under three hours, break for lunch, and go around again in the afternoon in under three hours. They play two rounds as fast as some of us play one round. In multi-day club events, playing foursomes one day makes a great change of pace.

The foursome format adds psychological burdens because you know your partner has to pay for your mistakes. You have to play to your partner's strengths and away from his weaknesses, rather than just play to your own strengths and weaknesses.

SKINS AND MORE

Skins matches are a lively change of pace. Halved holes can carry over until you wind up playing one hole for high stakes. You don't have to be the best player to win most of the money—just the luckiest. You can shoot the worst score of the day and win the most skins.

The key is to go over the scorecard in advance and come up with a hole-by-hole game plan to guide you. Figure out on the card which holes will be the hardest for you. If a hole doesn't play to your strengths, your goal will be just to halve it and get on to a hole where you have an advantage.

Or you occasionally could figure that nobody else is going to play the hole well either, so you might want to take a big risk and try to win it. You play cautiously until you get to that hole and then go for broke. But you plan that in advance. I usually play skins as an add-on to other competitions.

Stableford competition is just as unpredictable. You gain points based on your score for each hole. The modified version we use at the International Tournament in Colorado goes like this: A double eagle is worth eight points, an eagle five, a birdie two, a par zero, a bogey minus-one and a double bogey or worse minus-three.

The minus points ruin you. My attitude is that I have to avoid double bogeys, so I play conservatively when I get in trouble. I compare Stableford to when I first tried to qualify on Mondays for tour events. I could afford one double bogey in a round—but not two. That always was in the back of my mind: two doubles and I was down the road.

That kind of thinking affects your strategy in a Stableford, where two double bogeys cost you six points. It's too tough to get those back; you need three birdies. You don't take the extreme risks you take in match play. If you have a shot to a tight flag position with water nearby, you restrain yourself. You settle for a bogey before you run a risk that could cost you a double bogey.

The scramble is an increasingly popular format, with quite a few variations. All the players in a group drive off the tee, then they choose which ball to play for the second shot, third shot and so on into the hole. Typically everybody contributes during the round, even the poorest players, which is a great thing about the format.

The variation I prefer is that each player in a group must use his drive a minimum of three or four times. You don't want to come to the last tee with one of your drives unused and facing a long water carry. That's pressure!

CHAPTER 15
Playing Under Pressure

Early in my career I had a reputation as a choker. It was somewhat deserved. It took me a while before I could handle pressure when I was in contention to win. You have to get there and choke a few times to become a pressure player. It's part of the learning process every successful golfer goes through. We've all choked.

I was giving a clinic for weekend golfers not long ago, and someone asked me what I do under pressure—how I relax coming up to the last hole of a major championship with a chance to win. This man was intelligent enough to realize that the best players in the world get just as nervous playing tournament golf as you get playing for a couple of dollars.

When I feel myself tightening up under pressure, I shake my hands at the wrists like a swimmer who's on his mark ready to start a race. My dad taught me to do that when I was a kid, and it's always helped. A swimmer wants a feeling of freedom before the gun goes off. So does a golfer.

Try "shaking out" your hands preparing for an important shot. I often will do it before I putt. Any tightness in my body eases, so I can make my best effort without forcing the stroke.

GRIP THE CLUB LIGHTLY

Hold the club just firmly enough to control it. Tension in your hands can spread into all your muscles and make them much too tight. You won't turn well or develop enough clubhead speed. Maintain a consistent, light grip pressure from one shot to the next.

I suggest to people that when they are practicing they back off on their grip pressure until the club gets loose in their hands. Then increase the pressure just a bit, and that should be about right.

The source of pressure can be obvious—an important putt, a drive down a tight fairway, playing with someone you want to impress. Or the source can be so subtle you may not even realize its presence—a little wind in your face, remembering a bad shot you once played in a similar situation, or even a domestic or business problem lurking in the back of your mind.

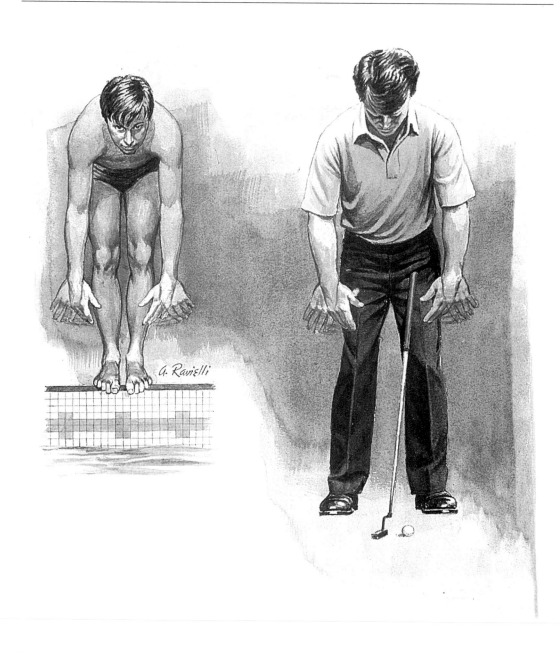

To relax, shake out your hands like a swimmer.

Whatever the cause, conscious or subconscious, it leads to some sort of physical reaction that creates the bad shot—a tightening of the hands and arms, a quickening of your swing pace, perhaps a laboring of the shoulders early in your downswing.

EXPECT SOME BAD SHOTS

One of the most common causes of undue pressure is expecting to hit perfect shots. This is unrealistic; the game is far too complex to allow perfection, or even near-perfection, no matter how skilled you may be. If you cannot abide bad shots, you are inflicting tension on yourself that will surely increase their frequency.

Walter Hagen, winner of 11 major championships, once observed that he expected to make seven mistakes per round. "When I make a bad shot," he said, "I don't worry about it. I figure it's just one of the seven."

I suggest you adopt Hagen's approach, as I did early in my career. Pick a number of shots that you might realistically expect to mis-hit to some degree over 18 holes, depending on your ability. Then, when you do make a bad shot, merely regard it as one of your quota. Forget about it and try to make your next shot a good one.

PLAY THE SHOT YOU CAN PULL OFF

No piece of advice, mechanical or mental, has ever benefitted me more than the words I received from the late Leland (Duke) Gibson shortly before I joined the PGA Tour. At the time, Duke was head professional at the Blue Hills Country Club in Kansas City, my hometown.

"Know what your limitations are," he told me. "Understand what you can and what you can't do. Never try to execute a shot under pressure that you are not capable of."

What Duke was saying was that I must know when to take a risk and when to play it safe. For example, if I have a little pop wedge shot over a bunker or water hazard to a pin cut close to the hazard, do I gamble with a tricky finesse shot to get it close, or do I merely get the ball safely onto the green? Some days you have a good touch with that shot, some days you don't. The decision on how to play it rests with my own knowledge of my capabilities and my limitations on any given day.

Every time I'm faced with one of these decisions, I remember Duke's words.

BREATHE PROPERLY

I've had doctors tell me this, and I believe them. Take deeper breaths before you play a pressure shot. Do breathing exercises to ease the tension. They will steady your emotions.

I've noticed that a great player like Lee Trevino yawns when he gets into a pressure situation on the course. It's a deliberate yawn that gives him oxygen and relieves tension. Under pressure your breathing becomes shal-

Lee Trevino likes to yawn to ease tension during a round.

low. Yawning forces air into your lungs and to your brain. It's like taking deep breaths when you're nervous, only better.

And I'll bet you're yawning now from the power of suggestion.

Performing under pressure is uncomfortable—accept that. Learn to thrive on pressure rather than be intimidated by it. Your adrenaline will flow more freely, which will make you quicker. Think in slow motion. Visualize your swing in slow motion. Slow down everything you do and you probably will be going at about normal speed.

Lanny Wadkins is a fast player, but when he knows he's in for a slow round he will slow his pace, especially walking from the tee to his ball. He doesn't want to hurry to his ball and then have to wait. The difference might be only 30 seconds, but it keeps him in a rhythm.

Golf is a walk in the park, not a 400-meter dash.

You need to find an internal pace that works for you as well as an external pace. You should strive to maintain a manageable state of excitement. You can't get too delighted over a good shot or too discouraged over a bad one. You need mental equilibrium—the fewer peaks and valleys the better.

Freddie Couples asked me about the mental aspects of the sport, and I told him you have to find the level of excitement at which you can play well. Then you have to try to keep it steady throughout the round. We're all human, so that level is going to fluctuate. But the less it does, the more consistently you'll perform under pressure.

RELY ON A ROUTINE

Consistency starts for me with practicing a preshot routine, which is the beginning of a series of movements leading into the stroke itself. Successful players rely on a precise routine that repeats itself automatically under pressure. They practice this routine until it becomes second nature.

An individual routine will vary from one golfer to the next—in the number of waggles, for instance—but a good golfer will use the same routine for every shot he plays. Lanny will take less time going through his routine than Nicklaus, but each will take that same amount of time prior to every shot he hits.

My routine begins once I've analyzed the shot and taken my practice swings. From then on I'm virtually on automatic pilot. My routine won't change from a drive to a tap-in putt. It consists of (in order) aiming the clubface on the intended line of the shot, taking my stance, looking at the target and then back at the ball, waggling the clubhead while looking at the target again, making one final waggle, then starting the swing.

The only time I interrupt my routine is if the wind changes or I'm distracted. If that happens, I'll start all over.

You will have to find the routine you're comfortable with and practice it until you can repeat it without even thinking about it. Your consistency comes from practicing that routine.

Once ingrained, your routine will ease you into pressure shots and help keep your nerves from acting up. If I see a player break his routine under pressure, I know he's in trouble. He hasn't practiced his routine enough to be confident in it.

Develop a consistent preshot routine, and your play will become more consistent under pressure.

WHAT TO DO WHEN THE WHEELS COME OFF

No doubt you know the abject frustration of losing your swing in the middle of a round. You've been playing well, but suddenly you lose your feel, one bad shot leads to another, and now you'd rather be home mowing the lawn or washing the windows.

A good way to regain your feel is to grip the club at the clubhead end and make a few practice swings. This makes the club very, very light. It gives you a refreshing sensation with your hands. When you go back to swinging the club normally, you'll be able to feel the clubhead, which is the most important thing you can try to do during the swing.

Swing the club gripping the clubhead end—and get the wheels back on. I've done it late in a tournament, and it's worked.

When I go bad during a round, I've learned the hard way not to think about swing mechanics as much as rhythm. I picture Sam Snead's languid rhythm in my mind, and that almost always helps.

Too often we get too conscious of mechanics, and forget that their place is primarily on the practice tee, not the golf course. We lose the visual sense of the shot and the distance. We should be trying to make contact and get the ball to the target the best way we can when we're struggling in competition.

Think about making a smooth swing. Revert to rhythm. That usually stops the bleeding.

And relax. As Dave Marr always told his uptight pro-am partners, there's no awful shot you can show him that he hasn't seen before.

CHAPTER 16
Tactical Shortcuts to Better Scoring

The pros don't have any big secrets for breaking par, but we do pick up little shotmaking gambits over years of practice and competition. Many times it's the quick tip that saves a stroke at an important time. On tour we all love to experiment and compare notes on different shots, from hitting a driver off the fairway to handling a left-to-right downhill putt.

I've put together here a collection of situational thoughts that require awareness more than power or finesse. Any alert player can apply them with a little extra practice. Most of them I've learned from my peers and am passing along to you in the hope they'll expand your arsenal of shots.

Don't ever attempt a shot on the course you haven't practiced. And don't ever stop learning new ways to cut your scores.

WHEN TO HIT THE DRIVER OFF THE GROUND

Hitting a driver off the fairway usually makes about as much sense as wrestling Andy Bean (who's used to wrestling alligators). But on dry, hard turf—dormant Bermuda grass, for instance—it can be a smart play.

Let's say you have a long second shot on a big par 5 or even a big par 4. Just swing smoothly and put the clubface on the ball. It will bounce and roll forever. Even a topped shot with a driver will go a long way when the ground is firm and the grass short.

Hitting a driver can be especially helpful if you're in the trees and have to keep the ball low and hit it far.

Don't try to catch the ball on the upswing with a driver off the ground. If anything, hit down on it a little. A metal driver, with its perimeter-weighted head, is easier to hit off the ground.

It sounds radical—but it can work.

FORGET YOUR WEDGE
ON THIS SHORT PITCH

What club would you use for a 40-yard pitch shot into a brisk wind with the pin in the back of the green? I'll wager you'd automatically take a sand wedge.

My choice would probably be an 8-iron.

The common failing is to come up far short, particularly if the green slants from back to front, the way most modern greens do. The wind knocks down your high wedge shot, and you get little or no roll.

Playing the 8-iron, I can beat the wind by swinging easier and imparting less backspin to the ball. The trajectory of the shot will be lower, and I can land the ball safely in the center of the green and run it back to the hole. I'll do this into any wind stronger than 10 miles per hour or a one-club wind. I try to make a smooth, normal half swing. It's mainly an arms swing, with little hand and wrist action. I don't punch the ball, because that would put too much backspin on the shot.

The wedge can be your worst club pitching into the wind.

TURN PUTTER SIDEWAYS WHEN BALL'S AGAINST FRINGE

Fred Couples and some other tour pros are using a new shot when the ball is snuggled up against the greenside collar. They turn the putter 90 degrees and hit the ball with the toe end.

The theory is that there's less blade to catch in the fringe grass. The toe end of the putter slices through the grass like an arrow. Because the heel sits higher than the toe when the putter is turned, the putter doesn't get caught in the edge of the fringe going back.

You need a putter with a fairly wide, flat tip if you're going to hit the ball off the axis line of the toe. And, like any unusual shot, this one requires some practice before you try it during a serious round. Use your normal putting grip and stroke, and the ball should roll like a putt.

LEAVE THE FLAGSTICK IN—AND TRY TO HOLE CHIP SHOTS

I like to leave the flagstick in when I'm chipping. It's a good backstop if I hit the ball too hard, and it often helps my depth perception.

Even putting from the fringe, I prefer to leave the flagstick in. Especially going downhill, it can save me.

I will make an exception and remove the stick if it's made from a stiff material. Flagsticks come in different flexes. The ones in the British Open are really firm because they have to withstand strong winds.

Another chipping thought. Try to hole your chips. It's been my experience since I was a kid learning to play that if you try to sink a chip shot, you get closer to the hole. And occasionally you make one.

DEALING WITH DEEP FAIRWAY BUNKERS

When I think of Muirfield, where the British Open was played in 1992, I think of the penal bunkers. You never can reach the green out of a fairway bunker there, and sometimes you have to come out sideways or backward.

The bunkers are even bigger than they look, because the hard ground all around them slopes right into them.

On a long hole like the par-5 17th you need to advance the ball as far as you can if you get in the horrendous cross bunkers. You have to hit a high shot with as strong a club as possible.

My keys are to open the clubface quite a bit and set my hands behind the ball. I also aim left.

The smart play is to avoid a penal bunker if at all possible.

CHANGE BALL POSITION
TO PLAY ENOUGH BREAK

Weekend golfers underplay breaking putts and tour pros overplay them. The faster the green, the more the ball is going to break. You will wind up closer to the hole more often if you overplay the break. Keeping the ball on the high side of the cup—or the "pro side" as it's called—will help it die down to the hole.

Changing the ball position in your stance can help on breaking putts. Generally the ball should be just ahead of the center of your stance. From there, try moving the ball one ball forward in your stance for left-to-right putts, and moving it one ball back in your stance for right-to-left putts. You'll have a better chance of playing enough break.

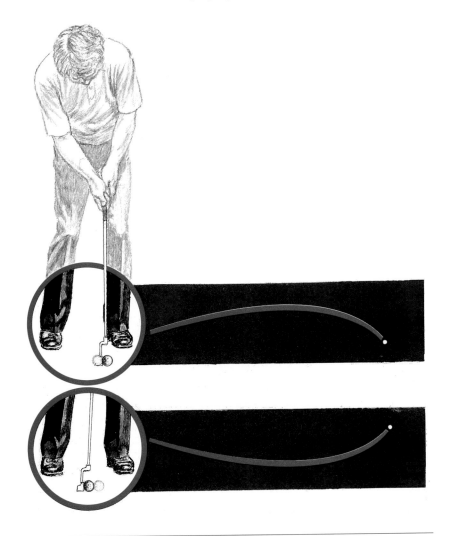

HIT THE GRASS-AGAINST CHIP
50 PERCENT HARDER

How many times have you flubbed a chip shot when the ball is sitting down in rough grass with the grain against you? It's a tough little shot.

Most players fail to get the club through the ball because the grass stops the club quickly. They come up far short of the hole.

They think they've misplayed the shot, but actually they've just misjudged how hard to hit it. You have to make yourself hit this shot 50 percent harder than a normal chip. Not 10 or 20 percent harder—50 percent harder!

I use a wedge and put the ball back at least in the middle of my stance, with my feet and the clubface slightly open. I take the club up more abruptly than usual on the backswing, to avoid as much grass as possible. Then I swing through the ball with a firm left hand and hit it 50 percent harder!

WHEN THERE'S MUD ON THE BALL

Despite what your friends may tell you, the Rules of Golf don't allow mud to be removed from the ball until it's on the green. Sometimes we play a local rule on tour that allows us to "lift, clean and place" a muddied ball. If that isn't in effect, you've got to play the ball as it lies.

I've heard tour players say the ball will curve left if mud is on the left side of the ball, or curve right if mud's on the right side of the ball. I haven't found that. If anything, I've seen the ball curve one way and then try to correct itself and curve the other way—it might hook and then slice.

When there's mud on the ball, I play well away from hazards. I aim straight, don't try to maneuver the ball and play a more cautious shot than usual.

USE LESS LOFT FOR PITCHES
INTO UPHILL GREENS

A friend of mine, a 12-handicapper, was about 60 yards from the green after one of his better drives. The deep green sloped dramatically from back to front, and the hole was cut toward the back. My friend made a fairly full swing with a sand wedge. The ball landed softly, died into the slope and finished well short, down in three-putt territory. Like most golfers, he had underjudged the effect of the green's contour on the ball's bounce and roll.

I told him the better percentage play in that situation is to hit a three-quarter pitching wedge. Because the club has less loft, the ball will land about the same place as the sand-wedge shot, but will roll up to the hole.

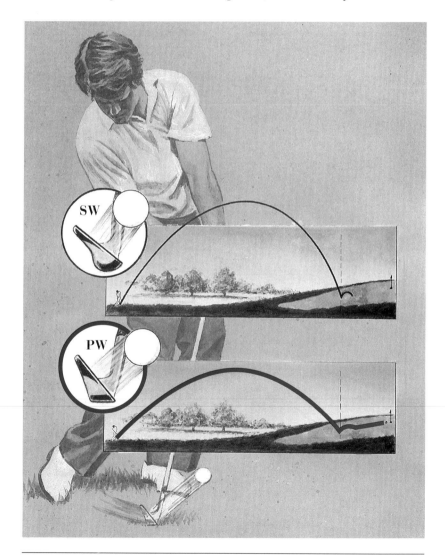

WHAT TO DO WHEN THE BALL SITS UP HIGH

A reader asked me recently what I do when the ball is sitting up in tall grass. It's a tricky lie—I've seen good players swing under the ball and never touch it. I rely on two keys, whether it's a short shot or a long one.

First, I make the club shorter by gripping down toward the steel. It's like a sand shot, where you grip down because your feet are dug into the sand. Here you grip down because the ball's up higher than usual.

Second, I address the ball with the clubhead off the ground. You tend to swing the club back to its original position. Also, you won't risk moving the ball accidentally as you address it, and you won't cramp your extension.

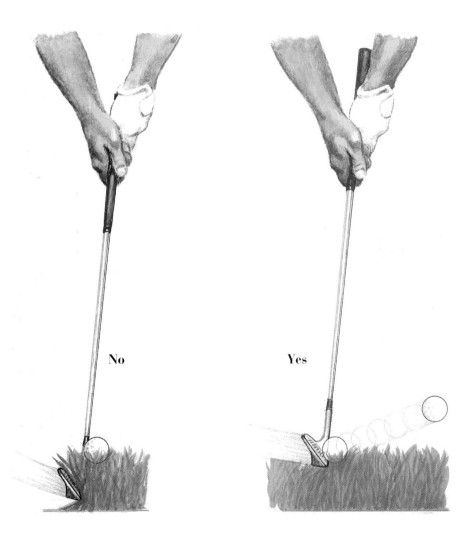

No   Yes

MOVE THE BALL FORWARD ON
LEFT-TO-RIGHT DOWNHILLERS

The most fearful putt in golf is downhill and left to right. It's easy to lift up your body and swing the putter to the right, which results in a feeble effort that never has a chance of going in.

I make one small adjustment when I face a left-to-right downhiller. I move the ball an inch forward in my stance. I play the ball off my left instep instead of my left heel.

That helps me start the ball on line or even a little left, from where it still can fall in the hole on the high side. I try to keep the putter on the intended starting line of the putt through impact and into the follow-through.

My hands and arms stay in their normal positions even though I move the ball an inch forward. Nothing you do makes a downhill, left-to-right putt fun, but I've found that this gambit takes some of the fright out of it.

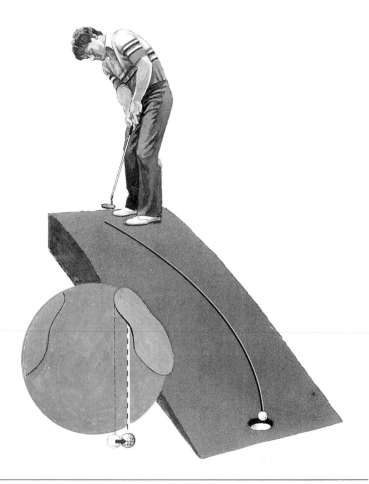

CHAPTER 17
Your Options to Consider

Let's see how you can apply what you've learned to that situation I posed for you in chapter one. (It's reshown on the next two pages.) You were in the left side of the fairway, 200 yards from the flag, remember, with 170 yards to carry the hazard and 60 yards to the left fairway bunker.

What are your options? You have two main ones: to go for the green or to lay up. Then you have sub-options in each case.

If you feel you can clear the hazard comfortably, your obvious best sub-option is to hit the green. Your obvious worst option going for the green is to hit the ball in the hazard on the left. The right or left greenside bunkers aren't bad places to be, if you're a good bunker player. But if you miss to the right of the right bunker you are going to have an extremely difficult shot from a severe downslope—even to get the ball on the green, much less near the hole.

If you decide to lay up, think of playing two 100-yard shots. Your best choice is to aim just to the right of the hazard stakes, toward the right side of the fairway (don't go too far right or you will have to approach the green over the right greenside bunker).

It's important to realize that you will not be laying up straight at the green with this choice. With the flag on the front, you should aim to the right of the offset green. You will position yourself to play your next shot, of another 100 yards or so, straight up the axis or length of the green. On this ideal line, you avoid having to carry the ball over any trouble. You give yourself the option to play a low-running approach shot, landing the ball short and rolling it up to the front flag position, or the option to carry the ball and stop it on the green. This first lay-up position is the best because it's the least difficult and runs the lowest risk against success. (It would be an even better choice if you were playing the hole downwind and needed to bounce and run the ball up the axis of the green.)

Your second best lay-up choice is to go straight for the flag, leaving the ball short of the fairway bunker and the water hazard. This position is less desirable than position No. 1 because it forces you to hit over the water

**Lay up
Choice No. 3**

**Lay up
Choice No. 2**

hazard and because the angle of your approach shot cuts off much of the landing-and-roll area you need to keep the ball on the putting surface. You have to be more accurate with your approach, increasing your risk.

A point I might mention here is that most golfers, from the best pros

Lay up Choice No. 1

to the worst hackers, tend to laugh at the idea of hitting a 100-yard lay-up shot. The macho factor sandbags them. Because the lay up is so short, they think they have to go for the green, notwithstanding the risk. Usually they wind up wishing they'd taken a good, easy lay-up route instead.

Your third best lay-up choice is to put the ball in the fairway 20 yards left of choice No. 2, over the fairway bunker but short of the water hazard. Even though your ball is in the fairway, you have further tightened the effective landing-and-roll area on the green for your next shot, forcing yourself to attempt an extremely difficult carry. If your lie isn't good, and you are not a good wedge player, your risk against success from this position is too high and you won't be able to hold the green.

When you come to a hole like this, remember that golf is similar to chess and pool in that *you must always think from where you want to play your next shot.*

When you have the course to yourself some time, try playing two balls for your second shot whenever you get in a risky situation like this. Play a totally safe shot with one ball. With the other ball, gamble and run the risk. See how your scores compare. Or play a round where you hit two tee balls on every driving hole, one with a 5-wood and one with a driver. See what happens. You may be surprised.

I hope the strategy I've outlined in this book will help you think better, score better, and enjoy this great game even more!